Thomas K. Johnson

**The First Step in Missions Training:
How our Neighbors are Wrestling
with God's General Revelation**

World of Theology Series

Published by the Theological Commission of the World Evangelical Alliance

Volume I

Vol 1   Thomas K. Johnson: The First Step in Missions Training: How our Neighbors are Wrestling with God's General Revelation
Vol 2   Thomas K. Johnson: Christian Ethics in Secular Cultures
Vol 3   David Parker: Discerning the Obedience of Faith: A Short History of the World Evangelical Alliance Theological Commission (in preparation)
Vol 4   Thomas Schirrmacher (Ed.): William Carey: Theologian – Linguist – Social Reformer
Vol 5   Thomas Schirrmacher: Advocate of Love – Martin Bucer as Theologian and Pastor
Vol 6   Thomas Schirrmacher: Culture of Shame / Culture of Guilt
Vol 7   Thomas Schirrmacher: The Koran and the Bible
(This book is also available in German and Turkish) Vol 8   Thomas Schirrmacher (Ed.): The Humanisation of Slavery in the Old Testament
Vol 9   Jim Harries: New Foundations for Appreciating Africa: Beyond Religious and Secular Deceptions
Vol 10   Thomas Schirrmacher: Missio Dei – God's Missional Nature
Vol 11   Thomas Schirrmacher: Biblical Foundations for 21st Century World Mission

Thomas K. Johnson

The First Step in Missions Training: How our Neighbors are Wrestling with God's General Revelation

WIPF & STOCK · Eugene, Oregon

Wipf and Stock Publishers
199 W 8th Ave, Suite 3
Eugene, OR 97401

The First Step in Missions Training
How our Neighbors are Wrestling with God's General Revelation
By Johnson, Thomas K.
Copyright©2014 Verlag für Kultur und Wissenschaft
ISBN 13: 978-1-5326-5358-2
Publication date 3/15/2018
Previously published by Verlag für Kultur und Wissenschaft, 2014

"In a time when Euro-American culture has lost confidence in its rich heritage, we need more than ever a work such as this by a theologian such as Thomas Johnson. This should be required reading in every seminary and graduate program that deals with the meaning of culture."

Gerald R McDermott
Jordan-Trexler Professor of Religion
Roanoke College, USA

"A stimulating discussion of the problems of general revelation – particularly designed for those engaged in the missionary task."

Dr John Warwick Montgomery
Professor Emeritus,
University of Bedfordshire, England

"A must read for all Christian students in higher education. Prof. Johnson provides a biblical framework for the foundational philosophical questions that every person wrestles with and the lacking but all-framing theological idea for my own worldview. This book will contribute to the long needed reversal in apologetics: from defense to offense!"

Daniel Ellenberger
Director,
Martin Bucer Seminary, Zurich, Switzerland

"This important new book by Thomas K. Johnson casts new light on the meaning of Romans 1. By treating the passage as a missions training manual, he draws out surprising new interpretations for evangelism and apologetics. Johnson shows how we can join Paul in being proud ('not ashamed') of the gospel, full of confidence that it continues to speak to the human condition even in a postmodern age."

Nancy R. Pearcey
Director, Francis Schaeffer Center for Worldview and Culture
Professor and Scholar in Residence, Houston Baptist University

"This is a significant book on one of the most important subjects confronting Christians today: How to bring the biblical message to a world that thinks this message is meaningless or dangerous? Thomas Johnson's exposition of Romans 1-2 is a highly needed resource on general revelation, clearly written, eye-opening, compelling. I recommend this book most strongly."

Ron Kubsch
Lecturer in Apologetics and Contemporary Theology
Martin Bucer European School of Theology and Research Institutes

"Prof. Thomas Johnson is a unique person, since he is first rate theologian, a well-read philosopher, and a missionary at heart. In this latest book he has borrowed from all three disciplines to form logical arguments for the evangelical position on revelation. His involvement with the WEA has been very much appreciated, as has his work in the doctoral program at Olivet University. His book will definitively have far reaching influences in the future."

William Wagner
Co-president, Zinzendorf School of Doctoral Studies
Olivet University, California

"Thomas Johnson has written an excellent book on a subject that is very important but so often ignored in recent Protestant theology. Johnson presents a clear introduction to Paul's teaching on general revelation in Romans 1-2 and shows, so crucially, why general revelation does not reveal the gospel of Christ but is absolutely foundational for understanding it. Johnson's years of experience in mission work and university teaching shine through as he winsomely explains how God's general revelation haunts the unbeliever and provides the Christian evangelist with many opportunities to speak with them of the true human condition. I strongly recommend this fine volume."

David VanDrunen
Robert B. Strimple Professor of Systematic Theology and Christian Ethics
Westminster Seminary California

Contents

Part I: Wrestling with God in the Book of Romans 9

Introduction 9

    Romans 1:16-2:5 (original translation) 14

Chapter One: The Human Condition 17

    The Content of General Revelation 21

    The Normal Human Response to God's General Revelation 22

    Internal Contradictions Resulting from Simultaneously Accepting and Rejecting God's General Revelation 25

    Religious Reversals 28

    Missions Training 29

Chapter Two: The Human Condition, part 2 31

    God's common grace is his call to repentance 38

    The Solution: Thoughtful Pride in the Gospel 43

Interlude on contemporary theology: representative distortions from the twentieth century that Christians must avoid in the twenty first century 45

Part II: Faith Seeks Understanding 51

A Missionary Philosophy of the Divine-Human Wrestling Match 51

Chapter Three: Angst and General Revelation 53

Chapter Four: Moral Angst 63

Chapter Five: Existential Angst 67

Chapter Six: Ontological Angst 73

Chapter Seven: General Revelation and the Human Quest 79

Chapter Eight: Selected Questions in the Philosophy of Religion in
   Light of God's General Revelation 97
   A. Religions as Replacements 97
   B. General Revelation and "Proving God" 100
   C. General Revelation and Reason 103
   D. General Revelation and the Problem of Evil 106
   E. General revelation provides the background for perceiving
       special revelation and the reality of the Christian Life 108
   F. The Rejection of General Revelation and False Absolutizing 109
   G. Absolutizing within a Particular Field of Learning 110
   H. Conclusion: Who is wrestling with God's general revelation? 112

Appendices for students of theology and the humanities 115
   Appendix I: The Rejection of General Revelation and the Natural
       Moral Law in Twentieth-Century Protestant Theology 115
   Appendix II: Types of Beliefs 130
   Appendix III: The Missions Training Structure of the Epistle to the
       Romans 132

Questions for study and discussion 133

About the Author 141

Part I: Wrestling with God in the Book of Romans

Introduction

If you very seriously want to fulfill your calling as a missionary, to bring the biblical message to a needy world, what is the very first thing you should learn? Is it the language of the people you want to reach? Is it how to adjust to different cultures, where people really think differently and do things differently? Is it the history of the people you want to reach?

If you read the life of the apostle Paul, you might think the most important thing for a missionary to learn is how to swim very well, in case a few of the ships on which you are riding sink. (See 2 Corinthians 11:25.) Or maybe, following Paul, you will want to learn how to walk distances that seem long to us. (The distance mentioned in Acts 20:13 was 32 to 40 km, i.e., 20 to 25 miles.) Or maybe you should learn how to sing very joyfully, in case you are beaten and thrown into prison for preaching the gospel. (See Acts 16:16-39.) I have wondered if singing while being beaten was standard operating procedure for Paul.

What is truly astonishing is Paul's first theme when he wrote a manual on missionary training. In a very broad sense, the book of Romans was written by Paul as a missionary training manual, one of the earlier text books in history, designed to equip the church for its history changing task of bringing the gospel to the nations. He wrote it as an organic part of his missionary work, to explain his mission efforts to the church in Rome, to gain support from the church, and especially to train the entire church in Rome to become a missionary church. Of course, Christians have used the book of Romans for other purposes, perhaps as a source book for Christian doctrine or as a summary of theology, and there is nothing particularly wrong with these uses of the book. However, the arguments are convincing that Paul wrote his great epistle to the Romans to be a missions training manual, to help the church in Rome become a missionary church. You see this from the way the book starts, finishes, and is organized around the topic of the spread of the gospel to the entire world. The overwhelming theological, philosophical, and ethical content of the book does not stand alone;

it is set within the framework of world mission and is properly called a "Charter of World Missions."[1]

If this claim is true, then the book of Romans should again become central for missionary training. We want all our missionaries (which means all Christians!) to be able to say, with Paul, "I am not ashamed of the gospel," and to really know what they mean with these words, why they are convinced this is true, how this relates to human experience, and what kind of life flows from this message.[2]

What is truly astonishing is that the very first theme of the apostle, after his missionary framework (Romans 1:1-15) and gospel summary (Romans 1:16-17), is *not* the gospel. Paul's first theme is the divine-human conflict which forms the background for all of human experience prior to faith in the gospel. This conflict has to do with God's general revelation, the human suppression of that revelation, God's wrath, and his common grace. Paul regarded understanding these truths about God and humanity as the first step to prepare the Christians in Rome to become effective missionaries who were proud of the gospel in relation to their multi-religious and multi-cultural society; this understanding is also strategically important for our time. Paul understood that the entire human race is wrestling with God

---

[1] Thomas Schirrmacher's observations bear repeating: "Paul wants to proclaim the gospel to all people without exception, regardless of language, culture, and ethnicity ('Greeks and non-Greeks,' Romans 1:14) as well as regardless of education or social class ('the wise and the foolish,' Romans 1:14)... .It is for that reason that he comes to Rome... . Romans 1:15 is not a superfluous introduction. Rather, it gives us the actual reason for composing the book of Romans, namely to demonstrate that the expansion of world missions is God's very own plan." Schirrmacher continues that it is the framework of Romans that confirms this missionary purpose of the letter. "The parallels between Romans 1:1-15 and 15:14-16:27 show that Paul does not lose sight of the practical missionary considerations of his letter during the entire epistle." Quotations from Thomas Schirrmacher, "The Book of Romans as a Charter for World Missions: Why mission and theology have to go together," a gift from the Theological Commission to the Missions Commission of the World Evangelical Alliance, distributed at the meeting of the Missions Commission, November 7, 2011. For his accompanying chart, see Appendix III.

[2] In the first decade after the end of communism in eastern Europe, I heard cruel jokes about missionaries, mostly related to the lack of training of a few. One joke was that all a missionary needed to know was John 3:16 and *The Four Spiritual Laws.* Another, from the side of Christians who survived generations of oppression, was that missionaries were the people the sending churches could not endure in their own churches, so they sent them out. Paul clearly set a much higher standard of missionary preparation.

prior to the time when anyone hears the gospel.³ Conflict with God is the central theme of human existence. Understanding this conflict, this wrestling match of the ages between God and humanity, is the first step toward serious missionary courage and power. Understanding this conflict also provides crucial intellectual tools needed by all Christians as missionaries.⁴ The human race is lost and is continually suppressing their God-given knowledge of God. Nevertheless, even when people suppress their naturally given knowledge of God, the created order of the universe continually impinges on human life and consciousness, so that human life is a continual wrestling match with God and his created order, regardless of the belief or unbelief of a person or culture.

A word of self-disclosure is in order. As a young man, I studied religions and philosophies in a secular university with a view to bring the gospel into the secular universities. Soon I came to the very painful conclusion that some of the evangelical apologetics I had learned did not stand up in light of the various cross currents which dominated the university, ideas which advanced students might call critical philosophy, post-modernism, or deconstructionism.⁵ If my previously learned weak apologetics was all I had intellectually, then I had to become ashamed of the gospel, the exact opposite of what Paul experienced. This realization forced me to ask how Paul could be so pointedly unashamed, really proud of the gospel, even though he was obviously aware of the various lines of secular and religious thought in his day, some of which were naively religious, while others were philosophically critical and skeptical. Learning from Romans 1 and 2 became a matter of personal spiritual survival as well as a matter of regaining thoughtful missionary zeal.⁶ But this experience was not only for me, since the philosophies and theories I encountered in the university represented similar ideas in many cultures. My experience may be similar to that of many other Christians. Understanding Paul's teaching on God's speech through creation, with the complex human response, offers answers that

---

[3] I am borrowing the image of Jacob wrestling with God, Genesis 32:22-30, to describe the human condition.

[4] The currently used division into chapters in the New Testament probably began in the thirteenth century; the place of the division between chapter 1 and chapter 2 of Romans might cause us to miss the continuity of Paul's teaching. In this book we are treating the first part of chapter 2 as a continuing part of chapter 1.

[5] Paul's description of humanity in Romans 1 and 2 is a type of deconstruction of thought and consciousness but without a trace of the nihilism often suspected in normal deconstructionism. Paul's deconstruction is theologically based.

[6] My personal study of Romans 1 and 2 was prompted by reading multiple books by Francis A. Schaeffer (1912-1984).

can change us all from being ashamed of the gospel to becoming confident in the gospel.[7]

To repeat: Paul's pride in the gospel, his intellectual courage in the gospel, and his missionary audacity were based on his understanding of the human condition before God. This is a condition of repressing God's general revelation, even though the entire human situation, including all of human experience, is made possible by a continual dialogue and conflict with God's word in creation. God's general revelation forms the hidden theological assumption for all of life for all people regardless of culture or religion, an assumption that is both used and denied at the same time by unbelievers as part of their conflict with God. Thoughtful missionaries (which we all should become) will make this otherwise hidden assumption explicit in their own understanding of life and the gospel; then we can use this understanding to present the gospel wisely and boldly.

A Pauline understanding of general revelation provides a theory of knowledge, a philosophy of culture, a system of social criticism, an evaluative philosophy of religion, a complex philosophical anthropology, and a foundation for social ethics, all as a framework for world missions. Paul's complete worldview was unlike most philosophical theories we encounter, but this total worldview gave him both courage and guidance to lead the nations to faith in Jesus. Paul's God was continually speaking through creation in a manner that no one can avoid and which is the foundation for all of human consciousness, life, and experience, even if people often *want* to avoid God's presence and speech. It seems like people cannot acknowledge it. For Paul, God's self-revelation through creation, even when denied and suppressed, is fundamental for all that makes us human, including our internal contradictions, and especially our irrepressible religious drives and hard-to-deny ethical knowledge. Because Paul understood the complex, continuous, and universal divine-human encounter, he was proud of the gospel, confident in the truth and importance of the gospel, while living in a world of many religions, cultures, and philosophies. Paul's missionary intellectual courage was a gift of God which came by means of understanding God's general revelation and the self-contradictory response of people in conflict with God.

It is my impression that even we Christians, not only atheists and adherents of other religions, sometimes neglect or ignore God's general word in creation, the word which eternally and continually precedes his special

---

[7] A continuing study of Romans 1 provided a crucial part of equipping me for 19 years of teaching ethics, religion, and philosophy in six secular universities in four different countries.

Word in Christ and in Holy Scripture; this weakness left me ill-equipped for our missionary calling, the main theme of Romans. This ill-equipped status can push us into either theological liberalism (which often appropriates a limited set of Christian truth claims on the basis of a philosophy of life, worldview, or narrative that is not biblical in its origin) or into extreme fundamentalism (which holds or presents Christian truth claims in an improper manner).[8] We easily adopt a fight-or-flight relation to culture, education, and politics, unintentionally advocating either an ethics of holy withdrawal from the world or an ethics of domination over the world. Our evangelism, preaching, and educational efforts are weakened because we sound like there is no connection between the biblical message and the rest of human experience. The gospel can begin to seem irrelevant or marginal in importance, even to Christians. Minimizing God's general revelation dishonors God and implicitly expresses ingratitude toward God.

On the other hand, if we think more deeply, if we really meditate on God's general revelation, we will begin to receive God's gift of missionary courage, including confidence in the truth of the gospel and a renewed understanding of the relevance of God's twofold revelation to all of human experience. For me, meditating about what God is doing (and has been doing throughout human history) in his creation, even before people hear the gospel, has become part of my worship to my heavenly Father, into which I invite you to join me.

This study will be in four major parts: 1) an original translation of Paul's manifesto in Romans 1:16-2:5, which includes some matters of technical exegesis in the translation; 2) "Wrestling with God: The Human Condition," which is a targeted exposition of selected themes in this particular text; 3) "Faith Seeking Understanding," a multifaceted study inspired by Paul's method of thought, including reference to other biblical texts, addressing missionary questions related to philosophy, religions, and ethics; and 4) some academic appendices.

The goal is to take the first step to prepare believers to become missionaries: understanding the condition of the unbelieving world, which is continually in self-conflict and in conflict with God: fighting with God's

---

[8] In the several varieties of what I am calling "theological liberalism," the biblical message is appropriated and interpreted in light of a previously accepted worldview or philosophy of life, which generally rejects the idea of an objective moral law, a central element in general revelation. Extreme fundamentalism treats the people to whom the biblical message is brought as if they have no previous encounter with God or knowledge of God that will play a role in how the gospel is accepted.

general revelation while also depending on God's general revelation and God's common grace, so that everyone is responding to that God in manifold ways. This can increase our intellectual and practical courage in communicating and applying the biblical message in the midst of a world that is never really secular.[9]

Romans 1:16-2:5 (original translation)

(16) I am not ashamed of the gospel, for it is the power of God intended for salvation for each person who believes, first for the Jew and then for the Greek. (17) In it the righteousness of God is revealed by faith and unto faith, as it is written, 'The righteous will live by faith.'

(18) For the wrath of God is being revealed from heaven against all the godlessness and injustice of men who suppress the truth by means of injustice, (19) since the knowledge of God is plain in them; for God has made himself known to them. (20) His invisible characteristics are received into consciousness through the creation of the world, namely his invisible power and divine nature, so that people are without an apology.[10] (21) Although they knew God, they did not glorify him or give thanks to him, but became worthless in their thoughts and their senseless hearts were darkened. (22) Claiming to be wise, they became foolish and (23) exchanged the glory of the immortal God for the image of the likeness of mortal man, birds, animals, and reptiles.

(24) Therefore God gave them over by means of the covetous desires of their hearts unto uncleanness to dishonor their bodies among themselves, (25) particularly the very people who exchanged the truth of God for a lie and deified and worshipped the creation in place of the Creator, who is blessed forever, amen. (26) Therefore, God gave them over unto dishonorable passions; for example, the women exchanged natural sexual relations for those which are contrary to nature, (27) as also the men left natural sexual relations with women and burned in their desires for each other, man for man, contrary to the scheme of nature; and thereby they receive in themselves the repayment which was necessary for their delusion.

---

[9] No bibliography and very few footnotes are included in this book, since that would unnecessarily extend its size and make it less accessible to readers. Implicitly, this essay is a dialogue with much of the history of theology and western philosophy, but to make that explicit at every point might exceed the patience of the reader and the writer. Some of this is in the appendices.

[10] Paul's term in Greek which I have translated as "without an apology" is a legal term, *anapologetos*, meaning "without a defense." This term situates the human race as the accused in God's courtroom. It has little similarity to our common apology, "sorry."

(28) And since they did not recognize the knowledge of God that they had, God gave them over to a confused state of mind, to do those things which are inappropriate. (29) They are full of envy, murder, strife, deceit, and malice. They are gossips, (30) slanderers, God-haters, insolent, arrogant, and boastful; they invent ways of doing evil; they disobey their parents; (31) they are senseless, disloyal, lacking in normal affections, and merciless. (32) They know the requirement of God that those who do such things are worthy of death, but they not only do these things, they also approve of those who do them.

(2:1) Therefore, you are without a defense,[11] O human, everyone who evaluates any actions as inappropriate; for whenever you evaluate, you also condemn yourself, for you do the same type of things which you evaluate negatively. (2) And we know that the judgment of God is based on truth when it falls on those who take such inappropriate actions. (3) Are you really being logical, O human, to think you will escape the judgment of God when you both give a negative evaluation of the actions of others and also do similar actions yourself? (4) Do you despise the riches of God's kindness, indulgence, and patience, claiming not to know that this kindness of God should lead you to change your mind? (5) By means of your hard and unrepentant heart you are storing up additional wrath for yourself at the day of the revelation of the wrath and just judgment of God.

---

[11] Here Paul uses the same key word as in 1:20, *anapologetos*, showing that he is continuing to explain the same theme.

Chapter One: The Human Condition

In Romans 1:16-2:5 Paul summarizes his assessment of the human condition without the gospel, which we are describing as wrestling with God's general revelation. Readers are encouraged to repeatedly refer to this text, and to the original translation of this text in the previous chapter, in order to consider it deeply. What follows is a targeted exposition of selected themes in this text that may be occasionally forgotten but which will enable believers to better grasp the condition of the people who need the gospel of Christ. Understanding the condition of people before God can equip Christians with missionary audacity.

Chapter Thesis: All of human life outside of the gospel is filled with the terrible contradiction of both knowing and not knowing God at the same time.

To understand Paul's conception of life before God, one has to see the human condition as filled with truly terrible spiritual, moral, and intellectual conflicts, contradictions, and tensions. At the center of these contradictions stands the problem that all people have a significant and content-rich knowledge of God, even though people without the Bible do not want to accept or acknowledge that they have this knowledge about God and from God. Everything that people say, think, and feel about God, morality, and other important topics arises out of their deep, primordial conflict with God. All that people do in all the areas of life and culture is involved in this wrestling match of the ages. Even the common claim of religious "neutrality," that one can talk about God in the same way one talks about minor everyday matters, is itself a product the human conflict with God, really an attempt to hide from God.[12]

Paul does not provide precise theoretical terminology, but he assumes a fundamental contrast between two types of knowledge of God. This contrast is between a deficient knowledge and a proper knowledge of God, which is also a contrast between a rejected knowledge and an accepted knowledge of God. The first type of knowledge is what all people have by virtue of creation and general revelation, whether it is called improper, de-

---

[12] Neutrality toward God is a modern myth spun by the sons and daughters of Adam and Eve in an attempt to cover up our status of being expelled from the Garden of Eden and in revolt against God.

ficient, or rejected. This first type of knowledge of God is inseparable from conflict with God. The second type of knowledge, whether it is called proper or accepted, comes only by the gospel. This second type of knowledge of God has to do with peace with God by faith in Jesus.[13] All people have some type of knowledge of God, whether improper or proper, rejected or accepted. This distinction is at the center of human experience and influences all of life, particularly in relation to God himself. God is unavoidable. This means the knowledge of God in the gospel assumes the previously rejected knowledge, but gospel-based knowledge of God does not build on the rejected knowledge of God, as if gospel-based knowledge is a second level that builds upon a lower level. The two types of knowledge of God are not like floors in a building, such that one stands on top of the other.[14] The knowledge of God we receive in the gospel radically changes and redirects the rejected knowledge of God, as well as adding to it. In the light of the gospel, we can acknowledge that we previously did not want to know God, even though he was making himself known to us through all of creation.[15]

Paul claims that God really is revealing himself through creation to all people on earth, and the language Paul uses is in two verb tenses, including the completed past and also the ongoing present. God effectively and sufficiently revealed himself through his initial work of creation at the beginning of time, and God is also actively continuing to speak through his creation to humankind throughout all of history. (In Romans 3:21 Paul uses similar terminology to describe the revelation of righteousness from God

---

[13] When a person comes to faith in Christ, that person has a status of peace with God, being legally justified before God, forgiven of sins, and adopted as a child of God. In a decisive sense, conflict with God has ended. But many believers do not fully appreciate their status of peace with God and do not yet live out their peace with God in daily life. We have to appropriate and learn to enjoy our peace with God in a process of intellectual, moral, and psychological growth.

[14] Occasionally Christians have talked as if the two types of knowledge of God are layers or levels, so that the knowledge of God received by special revelation builds on top of knowledge of God received by general revelation. This manner of speaking underemphasizes the way in which unbelief means rejection of God's general revelation. Therefore I do not recommend this two floor way of understanding the relation between general revelation and special revelation.

[15] When, in Romans 12:2, Paul tells believers to be "transformed by the renewing of your mind," this surely includes learning to acknowledge their previously rejected knowledge as coming from God in order to honor him properly. Obviously this must include giving thanks to God for his continuing preservation of human life by means of general revelation, the very thing which unbelievers, who do not glorify God or give thanks to him (1:21), refuse to do.

received by faith in Christ, thereby showing that there are two revelations from God with different contents and purposes.) God did not merely create the world and go into retirement (as some deists seem to think);[16] he is currently speaking to all men, women, and children, whether or not they want to listen to God or even claim to believe in God. And this speech of God to all of humankind, even when rejected, is crucial to understanding ourselves and our neighbors.

To avoid misunderstanding, one should notice that Paul sees this activity of God as coming before any human interest in knowing God or asking about God. God has spoken through creation and is now speaking through creation. This is the word by which God created the universe and by which he keeps the universe in existence. It is the condition that made existence and life possible and which still makes existence and life possible.

Christians have used several different terms to describe this work of God through his creation: general revelation, natural revelation, or creational revelation. (We will usually use the term "general revelation.") Each of these terms has certain strengths, since this revelation of God is general (to all people), coming through nature (including human nature), which is always understood to be God's creation. To repeat, Paul thinks this naturally given knowledge of God is received into consciousness by all people prior to the gospel as a primordial reality, not merely as a theoretical possibility, but this knowledge is rejected and suppressed, so that even unbelievers know God, though they also do not know God at the same time.

---

[16] One evening more than 30 years ago, I said something very stupid to Leslie, my wife. I said something like, "I don't think God is very active in our lives." Moments later I was struck by lightning while in our living room in Chesterfield, near St. Louis, USA. It did not take me very long to realize that though I was a Bible reading Christian, the way I talked about God was truly blasphemous and was rooted in my personal conflict with God. And slowly I came to the more painful realization that even an honest person without the Bible should not say something so stupid about God because God's general revelation teaches us about some of the things God is continuing to do for all of us. See the following section on the content of general revelation. Of course, few people are honest about what they know from either God's general or special revelations.

Short Definitions
1. General revelation: God's speech to humankind through all of creation, which both renders all accountable to God and simultaneously makes life and culture possible. This is also called "natural revelation" or "creational revelation."
2. Special revelation: God's speech to humankind in the Bible and in Christ which has its center in the gospel of the death and resurrection of Jesus to provide salvation.

Chapter One: The Human Condition

The Content of General Revelation

As Paul describes God's general revelation, it has a massive amount of content. It is not only a feeling of dependence or an awareness of something higher and holy, though this is surely included. Paul describes or alludes to at least seven distinct and specific aspects or dimensions of the content of God's general revelation in this text, though not all seven are described with equal clarity. These are the seven aspects or content areas which Paul teaches that all people know in a rejected or deficient manner prior to hearing the gospel:

1. the invisible power of God (verse 20);
2. the invisible deity or divine nature of God (verse 20), which may refer to God's moral nature or attributes;
3. the moral demands of God's law, the natural moral law (verse 32);
4. the natural, created scheme or pattern for life (verse 27), which alludes back to the mandates given to Adam and Eve in the Garden of Eden;
5. the awareness that people deserve punishment for their sins (verse 32);
6. an awareness of human dignity and of that which is honorable about and for people, since the ability to recognize actions which are inappropriate for humans assumes a primal awareness, perhaps not articulated in words, of the dignity both of the people acting and of those receiving the actions (verses 29-32);
7. an awareness of God's common grace, meaning that on a daily level people often know they receive good gifts from God while they also know that they deserve the wrath of God (verses 2:1-5).[17]

It can be truly astonishing for us to begin to consider how much of what we know, and that everyone knows, is known only because of what God is continually doing. This content is much richer than what has been called "ethical monotheism," a term scholars use to refer the common content the historical religions of Judaism, Christianity, and Islam. According to the

---

[17] There are other aspects of the content of God's general revelation, described in other biblical texts, that are assumed though not directly mentioned in Romans 1 and 2; these include the way in which God asks questions of humankind (seen in Genesis 3) and the way God has "set eternity in the heart of man" (Ecclesiastes 3:11). Some of these will be discussed in a later part of this book.

apostle Paul, there is a rich pattern of truth proclaimed by God through creation (as well as in the Scriptures). As proclaimed through creation, it forms the foundation and condition for all of human life and experience even when God and his general revelation are not acknowledged. Not to recognize that God's general revelation is the necessary condition for all of human life and experience is ingratitude toward God.

As a result of this general revelation, there is an important sense in which all people in all times and in all places know God and make use of this knowledge of God continuously. Paul says the knowledge of God is plain in all people and to all people (verse 19), and this knowledge is taken into the consciousness of all people (verse 20). This is what makes us human and distinguishes humans from anything else in the world.[18] Of course, there is also an important sense in which many people do not know God; this is what makes the gospel important. We are here considering the deepest self-contradiction and paradox of human experience: in this most important area of knowledge, a lack of knowledge is based on knowledge. People do not know God because they do know God. How can this be?

The Normal Human Response to God's General Revelation

Without the gospel, people normally do not like knowing God because God is frightening; all people are aware that they deserve God's wrath because they have not obeyed his moral law. This primordial knowledge of God is the basis for the most primordial and ultimate of human anxieties which influences all that people say and do. For this reason, this knowledge about God and from God is suppressed or repressed (Think of a psychological/spiritual defense mechanism.), with the result that people

---

[18] Surprisingly, this truth about humans is sometimes even recognized by atheists. For example the nineteenth century atheist philosopher Ludwig von Feuerbach (1804-1872), who thought that God is a projection of mankind's ideal character with no existence outside of human consciousness, nevertheless said, "Religion has its basis in the essential difference between man and the brute—the brutes have no religion." In other words, the difference between humans and animals is that humans are religious. See Feuerbach, *The Essence of Christianity,* translated into English by George Eliot, as excerpted in *Nineteenth-Century Philosophy, Philosophic Classics,* Vol. IV, 2nd edition, edited by Forrest E. Baird and Walter Kaufmann (Prentice Hall, 2000), p. 135. Feuerbach's book was originally published in 1841 in German as *Das Wesen des Christentums*. Christians can use Feuerbach's critique of religious projection to describe the religions and ideologies created by various people and cultures as part of hiding from God.

can easily say they do not know God, while, at the same time, they really do know God, while holding this knowledge in a rejected status. All people know something about his power, his deity, his moral law, the created order for life, and that people deserve punishment in relation to God. People have a God-given impression of human dignity and sense that they receive better than they deserve. But without the gospel, people "suppress the truth" (verse 18), driving it into the murky underground of culture and subconsciousness, though it continues to condition all we do and to repeatedly pop back into consciousness.

Psychologists sometimes talk about the suppression of memories or truths that are frightening or deeply disturbing; sociologists of knowledge talk about the way in which even supposedly objective scientific truth claims are heavily influenced by our fears and expectations. The idea that what people think is true and claim to know is not based on objective or pure reason is not a new idea; though not articulated in theoretical language, this idea is already present in the Bible. The general revelation that people deserve the wrath of God because of sin plays a decisive role in what people think they know. People pretend not to know truths they prefer not to know. The truth is too frightening.

One can take the account of Adam and Eve hiding from God behind a bush or tree as a metaphor for the history of the human race, including Paul's time and our own. (Romans 1:18-2:5 can properly be seen as an application of Genesis chapters two through nine, even if the book of Genesis is not directly quoted. There are numerous allusions to Genesis.) From our personal experience, one could think of the way small children imagine that if they cover their eyes so they cannot see other people, other people cannot see them; if people say they do not know God, they imagine that God does not exist or that God does not know them. Without knowing the gospel of Christ, it is too frightening to acknowledge that God knows us fully. Only when we grasp the gospel, that God is so gracious and forgiving that he sent his Son to purchase our redemption, can we then begin to recover from this illness of mind and soul that leads us to claim that we do not know God, when, in fact, all of us know God. It is terrifying to know we deserve the wrath of God. The default mode of consciousness of the human race is, therefore, to pretend we do not or cannot know God, often by means of creating a vast array of idols and views of God or the Ultimate which are not so terrifying or which can be appeased by our best efforts.

According to Paul's description of the human condition, our predicament is epistemological sin or epistemological injustice. This terminology requires explanation. If a witness in a criminal court trial does not tell the court all he or she knows about the crime under consideration, that witness will be guilty of a crime in the realm of knowledge. The witness does not publicly acknowledge all that he or she knows. Depending on the country in which the crime occurs, it may be defined legally as obstruction of justice or perverting the course of justice. This is an act of distinctly *epistemological* (related to knowledge) injustice. Something similar is happening continually in relation to God, though before God we do not have a right to remain silent to avoid incriminating ourselves. People say they do not know God, and they probably even say that to themselves, when they really do know God. This is lying, an act of injustice in relation to truth, so that it is not wrong to say that lying about God is the *fundamental* sin.

Unbelief always involves sin, is a result of sin, and is itself sin. One can say that unbelief is the core of original sin, in such a manner that the many sins of the flesh and sins in relationships, which Paul describes at length, flow from unbelief.[19] The center of the human problem is in the realm of what we claim to know or not to know; this is epistemological sin and injustice. For many centuries Christians have said that the sins of the spirit, such as pride and ingratitude to God, are deeper than the sins of the flesh and contribute to the sins of the flesh. What we learn from our renewed study of Romans 1, that lying about God is fundamental to sin, is complementary to this traditional observation. Paul already noted the internal link among the sins of the spirit: the people who deny that they know God also do not give thanks to him (verse 21), showing the internal spiritual links among ingratitude, unbelief, and lying about God.

A sin of this magnitude has significant results in the entire life of those guilty of the sin. Some of the results that Paul mentions are closely related to the arena in which the sin occurs, the internal life of the mind and soul.[20] He says, "... they became worthless in their thoughts and their senseless hearts were darkened. Claiming to be wise, they became foolish ..." (verses 21 and 22). One should not confuse cause and effect. Worthless thoughts, darkened senseless hearts, and claims of wisdom that cover up true foolishness are the result, not the cause. The cause is the epistemological sin of unbelief. People claim they do not know God when they really do know God. Their knowledge of God includes the entire rich and com-

---

[19] Unfortunately, coming to faith does not immediately and completely bring our sins of the flesh and sins in other relationships to an end. Paul still has to address such sins among believers in passages such as Romans 12:9 to 13:14.

[20] Here, and throughout Romans 1, Paul is describing "the pattern of this world" (Romans 12:2), from which believers are to be continually turning away.

plex content that everyone receives into consciousness from God's general revelation.

Internal Contradictions Resulting from Simultaneously Accepting and Rejecting God's General Revelation

Knowing God (in a rejected manner) when they claim not to know God is the reason that people often act as if they do not really believe what they claim to believe. A person may claim to be a complete moral relativist, saying that there is no universal moral standard or moral law, but then that person may shout that terrorism or racism is terribly wrong and may also feel horrible guilt inside; such people, who are very common, deny their own worldview by applying a known moral law to others and to themselves. A person may claim to be a complete skeptic with regard to all knowledge, saying we cannot be sure of knowing anything, but then that person acts as if we all have a lot of shared true knowledge; whether we are crossing a traffic-filled street or doing our banking, we all act on the basis of a lot of information we think everyone knows to be true. The anarchist may claim that all laws and governments are unnecessary, undesired, and harmful, but when his group is attacked by neo-Nazis on the street, the anarchist calls the police, wanting his freedom of speech to be protected by law. This step obviously makes the anarchist philosophy of life look like a game, not a serious conviction.[21]

Part of the time people act and talk according to their repressed knowledge, which they receive from God's general revelation, instead of acting according to the beliefs they claim to accept. (We can be grateful to God that many people do not practice the beliefs they claim to accept, since it leads to many good results for all of us. It is a dimension of common grace.) When a religion or ideology denies the truths which God proclaims via general revelation, its adherents do not fully believe their own words. They are of two minds, needing to trust the truths of general revelation in order to live, while they claim to affirm alternate beliefs.[22] This is the origin of the conflict most people have between their professed beliefs

---

[21] The anarchist described is a close friend before he came to faith; the other people described are composites of many students I have taught in various universities.

[22] The inner conflict of being of two minds explains much of the religious and ideological extremism we observe in society. Inner conflict or uncertainty easily leads to hostility toward people who profess other beliefs. Real peace with God leads both to becoming peaceful people and to courageous gospel proclamation.

and their practiced beliefs.[23] Paul's courage and pride in the gospel are related to how the gospel allows people who have become believers (and those on the way to faith in the gospel) to both accept and explain those truths which are in conflict with their professed beliefs and keep them from fully affirming and practicing their own professed beliefs.

It can be a significant step, both toward faith and toward intellectual integrity, when a person recognizes that he/she does not really believe his/her own philosophy of life and, in fact, lives on the basis of known truths that cannot be explained without reference to God and God's general revelation. Many fashionable religious and philosophical claims are in conflict with the truths (learned by general revelation) we all presuppose in order to carry on our lives. Identifying this conflict, this status of being of two minds, can be painful for a person, but we should attempt to assist people through this process. This internal contradiction is part of the common spiritual defense mechanism people build against God's general revelation. The gospel of forgiveness in Christ is the way out of this internal conflict and contradiction; as Christians, we can be of one mind within ourselves, with a real explanation of our experience; this is part of what we can tell people who are interested in the gospel.

---

[23] Among people who are not Christians, their practiced beliefs are often better than their professed beliefs because of the influence of God's general revelation. Among Christians, our practiced beliefs are often not as good as our professed beliefs because of the continuing influence of sin and unbelief.

A Personal Experience

Many years ago, when I was a nasty young lecturer in philosophy, I played a philosophical trick on a young woman in an ethics class I taught. She wrote a course essay in which she argued brilliantly that all ethical concerns were a matter of taste; just as some people like ice cream while others like candy, some people like one set of actions while others like another set of actions. It clearly followed from her essay that it is equally good to like genocide or to like protecting human rights. My nasty trick was to write on her paper, "Excellent essay; failure."

She was quite angry when she came to see me a few days later. "How can you fail me if I wrote an excellent essay?" she almost screamed.

I calmly responded, "It tasted good. Ethics is a matter of taste."

"But a good paper deserves a good grade!!" she huffed.

With a bored glance, I responded, "You convinced me. Everything is relative."

"BUT THERE ARE RULES!! GOOD PAPERS GET GOOD GRADES!! EVEN PROFESSORS HAVE TO FOLLOW THE RULES!!"

And then the light went on in her mind. Her anger at me showed her that she did not really believe the things she had written in her philosophy essay. She really thought (contrary to everything she had written) that we all know a lot about right and wrong and there are real standards of proper behavior that are different from matters of taste. I gave her a good grade for what she learned, but her whole relativistic philosophy of life was broken to pieces. Like most people, she not only believed in a standard of right and wrong (in spite of what she said she believed); she also knew that I knew the same standard of right and wrong, God's natural moral law. Her denial of a standard of right and wrong was only a fashionable game she was playing. By losing her game, she may have begun to recover her soul.

I wish I could claim that this philosophical trick was my own idea; honesty requires that I say I learned it from C. S. Lewis and Romans 1. This trick shows something important about our moral knowledge; with Lewis, I would claim it also shows something very important about ourselves and about the nature of the universe. Further, these truths about moral knowledge, our selves, and the nature of the universe are best explained by the biblical account of God, the moral law, and human fallenness.

Religious Reversals

The worthless thoughts, darkened hearts, and general foolishness described by Paul lead to a profound and ironic exchange or substitution: People try to replace the Creator God with something he created, thereby also reversing the human relation to the rest of creation. In verse 23 he explains, "… they exchanged the glory of the immortal God for the image of the likeness of mortal man, birds, animals, and reptiles, …" using words that echo Genesis 2, where humans were to name (from a position of authority over nature) and be responsible for the rest of creation. This means that people create substitute gods to try to replace the Creator, but by this process they also reverse their own relation to the rest of creation, imagining something in creation to be an authority over themselves.[24] Unbelief does not lead to people becoming "religionless;" unbelief in the Creator/Redeemer leads to all sorts of religions, even atheistic religions, though Paul's description would lead us to expect to find the worship of some aspect or dimension of creation below the surface of consciousness, even among people who claim to be atheists. People are unavoidably religious, even if they may claim not to be religious and say they cannot or do not know God. Paul's analysis leads to saying that the many philosophies, worldviews, and religions of the world all involve a substitute or replacement for God.

Paul's claims are an obvious echo of the invitation of the prophet Isaiah to compare God with idols, and God's promises with the promises people hope are coming from idols, leading to a discrediting of idolatry. (See Isaiah 44:9-20 and Isaiah 46:5-9.)[25] Isaiah expected people to perceive the deception and foolishness involved in idolatry and then to draw back to reaffirm their faith in the God of the Old Testament covenants. Of course, some of the ancient philosophers in Greece and Rome also ridiculed the polytheism of their day, regarding it as silly nonsense, but they lacked a

---

[24] One can view many addictions as a current example of a reversed relation to some substance, practice, or instinct which was given in creation. Instead of people being in a position of authority over that substance, practice, or instinct (as was described in the account of creation in Genesis), people place themselves below the authority of that dimension of creation.

[25] Using ridicule designed to make people think more seriously, Isaiah mocked, "No one stops to think, no one has the knowledge or understanding to say, 'Half of it I used for fuel; I even baked bread over its coals, I roasted meat and I ate. Shall I make a detestable thing from what is left? Shall I bow down to a block of wood?' Such a person feeds on ashes, a deluded heart misleads him; he cannot save himself, or say, 'Is not this thing in my right hand a lie?'" Isaiah 44: 19, 20.

compelling religious alternative and gospel.[26] Similar to the prophets and philosophers, Paul expects people to perceive the foolishness and lack of credibility of the many forms of idolatry. His message explains both idolatry and why people can become serious critics of idolatry in a manner which makes Paul's gospel worthy of attention and consideration.

People are constantly creating new gods, and Paul's language suggests a wide diversity of substitute religions. Sometimes people imagine gods or goddesses that are images of themselves, perhaps idealized or tragic images of themselves, as seen in many types of polytheism. Sometimes people imagine a god or gods that are similar to something else in creation, as seen in various nature religions and fertility cults. Sometimes people create a god from a falsified and absolutized dimension of social experience, such as race, history, nation, or economic relations, leading to many social/political ideologies. The history of western thought portrays a series of "Gods of the Philosophers," each of which has only a few characteristics of the biblical God and is surely both less frightening than Paul's God and not a source of a real gospel of forgiveness of sin. Whether the philosopher's god is created by a deist, a pantheist, or a representative of some other philosophical orientation, it, he, or she is not the God who exercises both wrath and grace in both nature and history. The "Gods of the Philosophers" and the gods of the religions are projections arising from the divided minds of people who are suppressing the general revelation of the God of creation and redemption.

Whatever the type of substitute religion people develop, unbelief in the known but denied Creator drives people to replace him with something that attempts to explain the universe and also seems to promise the hope, comfort, meaning, forgiveness, reconciliation, and direction that only God can provide. Primal Angst in view of the known but denied law and wrath of God makes irreligion truly impossible. Paul sees human life as filled with self-deception on a scale that few other people have imagined, and at the core of that self-deception is a wide-ranging set of substitute religions and a denial of the only God to provide a real gospel. This makes preaching that gospel truly urgent.

Missions Training

When the apostle Paul preached to people without the Bible in Athens (Acts 17:22-34), he first mentioned a reference to an "unknown God" in

---

[26] Here I am thinking especially of Socrates and Plato.

their community, but then Paul immediately assumed that the people of Athens both knew a lot about this God and also had a conflict with God at the center of their lives. His audacious preaching was empowered by knowing the truths we have just studied. Even before Paul arrived in Athens, the people of Athens were wrestling with God.

The central internal conflict within human life is that of both knowing God and not knowing God at the same time because, without the gospel of Christ, people usually repress and attempt to avoid God's general revelation which is filled with rich, complex content. People are dreadfully afraid of God's general revelation because it includes the truth that we deserve God's wrath for our sins, but this ongoing revelation provides the necessary condition for all people to live as humans and to remain human. Therefore, people without the gospel are always of two minds, not really believing all the things they claim to believe, while they create all sorts of God-substitutes. Should we not be proud of the gospel, which allows us to understand our experience of the world and also gives us substantial hope?

Chapter Two: The Human Condition, part 2

In this chapter we continue our targeted exposition and application of themes from Romans 1:16-2:5. Readers are again encouraged to read the biblical text carefully, including the original translation of this text which appeared in the first chapter of this study. Readers should also refer back to the previous chapter which explained some of the ways in which human life without the gospel of Christ is characterized by the terrible internal contradiction of both knowing and not knowing God at the same time. Even when people claim not to know God, they continue to wrestle with God, and that wrestling match is the most important factor in the life of individuals and communities. The rich and complex content of God's general revelation, which all people receive into consciousness, makes it possible for humans to live as humans, even though the normal human response is to repress God's general revelation from our consciousness because it is truly frightening if we do not know the gospel. This understanding of God's general revelation and the human response should help equip us with missionary audacity. We have the privilege of bringing peace into the divine-human conflict.

In this chapter we present two main theses:

I. Though people may deny it, conflict with God is a central and defining characteristic of human existence.

II. God's common grace is his call to repentance.

An understanding of these theses derived from Paul's missions manifesto should help the Body of Christ, which in its entirety is a mission agency in which every Christian is a missionary, to become much more courageous.

I. Though people may deny it, conflict with God is a central and defining characteristic of human existence.

Unbelievers are guilty of a twofold substitution or replacement in their confrontation with God. The first part of this substitution, though already explained at length, bears repeating. People replace the truth about God with a lie. This is the truth that comes from God and is about God. It includes the knowledge of the demands of God's natural moral law, the knowledge of the created moral order for human life, the knowledge that we deserve God's wrath for our sin, and the knowledge that we frequently receive better than we deserve. The lie which replaces the truth about God is that one can be truly wise without God, or that denies the power of God, or that denies his moral demands and creation order. The second part of this substitution or replacement is the worship of creation or some dimension of creation in place of God. If people are internally compelled to worship something, and if they are unable to worship God without knowing the gospel, it is unavoidable that people will worship something from creation or an imagined image of something created. Idolatry flows from conflict with God.

In this conflict with God at the center of every person's life, God does not remain passive or inactive. If we think God is inactive, it is only because we misunderstand his activity. This theme bears repeating: the God of the Bible is never passive or inactive. God's response to the way in which people suppress their knowledge of God's general revelation is a response that should worry us profoundly: to give people over to their sinful desires. Paul repeats this terribly disturbing claim in similar terms three times (verses 24, 26, and 28). This means that God lets people experience some of the results of repressing their knowledge of God already in this life. In verse 24 Paul uses terms that echo the tenth of the Ten Commandments, which forbids coveting (having desires that are inappropriate). God lets people go into their own coveting and thereby into the self-destructive sins that flow from unrestrained coveting. In verse 26 Paul says that God gives people over to dishonorable passions.[27] In verse 28 Paul says that God gives people over to a confused state of mind. These are three complementary descriptions of the same set of acts of God, using literary parallels similar to those used in Hebrew poetry for the purpose of emphasis and content-rich explanation.

What unites these three descriptions is the claim that God repays the act of people dishonoring God (by not accepting their knowledge of him) by allowing people to dishonor and destroy themselves. In this way there is frightening but pure justice in the repayment. Dishonor to God is repaid by means of dishonor to humanity. To bring about this type of justice God does not need to intervene from outside by a special act. God does not always use a lightning bolt or a war to execute his wrath; God repays dis-

---

[27] The Bible does not say that strong passions or desires are wrong. There are times when our passions for good goals are not strong enough.

honor by allowing people to dishonor themselves assuming that people know something about human honor and dignity from God's general revelation. Sin is here conceived to be self-punishing, self-destructive, and self-dishonoring, though God gives people over to this process. Skepticism regarding the wrath of God, which is common, may arise because we assume that his wrath can only be implemented in a spectacular manner, not in processes of self-destruction or social decay which we too easily regard as "normal."[28] If we understand the wrath of God in the way in which Paul describes it, we will begin to perceive the wrath of God all around us all the time.

A key assumption in this act of God, not always noticed by readers, is that there are proper ways for people to honor themselves, namely by recognizing the truth of God and living according to his plan for his creation. When people accept their status as image bearers of the Creator, placed in this world to fulfill his mandates, there is honor for all; when people create god-substitutes in their own image or in the image of some other part of creation, there is dishonor for all, including self-destruction. Much of what Paul says about sinful actions in this text can best be understood as ways in which people dishonor or debase themselves, because God lets them do so. The inappropriate actions and characteristics described in verses 29 through 31 (e.g., greed, gossip, slander, insolence, arrogance, boastfulness, faithlessness, heartlessness, and ruthlessness) dishonor both the person acting and the people who receive such inappropriate actions. Appropriate human actions and characteristics are both honorable in themselves and express honor to the people receiving such actions.[29]

The assessment of the human condition in Romans 1 builds on a theme from the prophet Jeremiah, though Paul adds a significant development. Jeremiah preached that the people of Judah had exchanged the God who had spoken to them in the Mosaic Law for various types of idols, including trusting in the governments of Egypt or Assyria, instead of trusting in God. As punishment for this sin of exchange, God was allowing the people of Judah to experience the consequences of their sin (see Jeremiah 2). The

---

[28] As Christians we should learn to distinguish between God's ultimate works of judgment, at the end of history and into eternity, and his penultimate or secondary judgments, which occur in this life.

[29] It follows that it is an act of God's common grace when he restrains human sin, often by means of the process of social or individual moral evaluation, so that sin does not unfold to its full self-destructive and self-dishonoring end. This understanding of common grace contributed to Paul's missionary preaching and will be explained below.

development from Jeremiah's teaching to Paul's teaching is that Paul says people from all nations exchange the God who has spoken through his creation for all sorts of idols, for which God allows people very broadly to experience the consequences of their sin.[30] The principle, which Jeremiah applied to Israel in light of God's deliverance of the people of Israel from Egypt, is applied to the entire human race by Paul in light of God's general revelation to the entire human race.

Paul's teaching on homosexuality serves as a particular example of self-dishonoring. He claims homosexual desires and actions arise from a darkened heart and mind, a heart and mind that are or were deeply alienated from God and God's creation order.[31] There is a knowable scheme or pattern of nature, a created order that all people know they should follow, though this knowledge may be deeply suppressed, as all of God's general revelation may be deeply suppressed. Paul expects that all people naturally know the creation mandate that they should "be fruitful and multiply" as stated in Genesis 1, and that sexuality and the desire for intimate bonding is closely associated with this fundamental human mandate. Actions and desires contrary to this scheme of nature will be self-dishonoring, assuming that actions which correspond to the scheme of nature will be self-honoring. This means there is something deeply honorable and humane about marriage and childbearing. Though homosexuality could be described as sin, it can also be described as a variety of self-punishment for the sin of disbelief and rejection of God's created order and mandate.

A similar principle of understanding applies to the entire list of sins in verses 29 through 31, many of which allude back to the Ten Commandments. (Unrestrained coveting leads to breaking all of God's commands.) Any of the sins in this list, such as greed, gossip, slander, insolence, arrogance, boastfulness, faithlessness, heartlessness, and ruthlessness, can be explained using the same painful detail which Paul used in regard to homosexuality. The confused state of mind and heart resulting from rejecting God leads people to do all sorts of things that are inappropriate, meaning contrary to the honor or glory of those who bear the image of the Creator.

---

[30] There are also significant echoes of themes from the Old Testament book of Proverbs in Paul's description of sin as self-punishing and self-destructive. In the language of Proverbs, sin is foolishness, and foolishness is often self- destructive.

[31] Desires and habits that arose from alienation from God and God's creation order do not always immediately disappear when people are reconciled to God. For this reason the New Testament epistles are filled with instructions intended for believers who are engaged in a long term process of taking off one set of actions and habits and replacing them with renewed actions and habits.

The problem is not primarily that people do not know that these actions and vices are wrong; people know that they are wrong and know that these actions are condemned by their Creator. But their actions arise from their confused state of mind arising from unbelief, not from what they know (but partly reject) about what is truly right and wrong. The confused condition of people can go so far that they not only do what they know to be wrong; they sometimes even begin to excuse or condone those wrong actions which they know to be wrong.

Especially in verse 32 ("They know the requirement of God that those who do such things are worthy of death.") there is a development of an Old Testament theme, of which Amos 1 provides a good example. Amos preached a call to repentance to the nations surrounding Israel, specifically and graphically describing atrocities such as human trafficking and terrible war crimes, assuming that all people already knew that such crimes were terribly wrong. The preaching of Amos did not add new moral information, as if the people did not know that crimes against humanity were wrong, but his preaching made it much more difficult for his neighbors to repress the moral knowledge they already had. And his preaching increased the intensity of their awareness of the wrath of God which they deserved for their sins. In a similar manner, Paul explicitly says people know both the content of God's natural moral law and also that they deserve God's wrath, though this knowledge can be so deeply repressed people say they do not know. He then talks about these themes in a manner designed to increase their level of moral and spiritual discomfort with their repressed knowledge. Paul describes the way in which humans are wrestling with God in a manner that seems designed to move that wrestling match from being something that is hidden behind a tree or deep within human subconsciousness to become a matter of open discussion.

The most extreme form of human internal deception occurs when people not only practice evil but also "approve of those" who perform such evil actions (1:32). This is the point of calling evil good and calling good evil. By the way he created us, God gave us the ability to distinguish between good and evil, along with the knowledge that we must do the good. These deepest moral principles were written into human reason, emotions, and relationships when God created us in his image. (The first sin, with the tree of knowledge of good and evil in Eden, brought the experience of and encounter with good and evil, not the ability to distinguish between good and evil.) By his continuing general revelation, God constantly renews our knowledge of the difference between good and evil and reminds us of our duty to do that which is good and to avoid doing evil. When people deny the entirety of this God-given knowledge, they demonstrate that God has truly "given them over" so that they stand on the very edge of the abyss; hell is beginning to intrude into earthly existence. Normal social problems turn into genocide, the war of all against all, or the collapse of communities. Exactly when people imagine they have defeated God by obliterating him and his law from consciousness, they and their neighbors become the real losers, bringing destruction on earth, time and time again.

> **Definition: The Natural Moral Law**
>
> Already in ancient Greece and Rome, thoughtful and responsible people noticed that some actions were wrong, whether or not these actions were forbidden by social custom or civil law. Many said that the standard for recognizing such wrong actions is the natural moral law or the law of nature. Christians adopted this term and sometimes distinguished this natural moral law (which they saw as coming from God) from the "supernatural moral law" which God gave in the Bible. This terminology assumed we can usually recognize the difference between nature as intended by God and nature as it is distorted by sin.
>
> The terminology of "natural law" is not in the Bible, but the reality of the natural moral law is assumed throughout the Bible. If we want to update our terminology, one could suggest "universal moral law" or "general principles of equity" in place of "natural law." When used by Christians, the term "natural moral law" refers to the general revelation of God's law coming to us via nature which is God's creation. It was written by God into our minds, hearts, and relationships in creation and is a central part of general revelation, though sin makes people want to reduce or ignore it and especially to deny the source of the moral law. It is knowledge of the natural moral law, even if partly mistaken, which allows people of many nations to write civil laws which, at least in part, restrain some sins, promote order, and protect justice and human well-being. Though some disagree, I think Paul referred to the old Greek and Roman ideas of the natural moral law in Romans 2:14 when he mentions "Gentiles, who do not have the law, do *by nature* things required by the law (emphasis added)."
>
> One of the demands of the natural moral law is that we protect the well-being of our neighbors, assuming there is a general revelation of the dignity of human beings. Using the language of our time, this means we have a duty to protect "human rights." Though the language of "human rights" has sometimes been used inappropriately, we can talk about many demands of the natural moral law in the language of protecting the rights of others.

Like all the truths revealed by God's general revelation, awareness of the value or dignity of the lives of others can, of course, be suppressed by an individual or a culture.

There are several other moral languages, other than "human rights," which we can use to discuss and communicate the demands of God's natural law today. These other moral languages include matters such as the need for moral character, considering the personal and social consequences of our behavior, what contributes to the human good, and what principles we can reasonably expect all people to follow. When people describe their awareness of their sins, they often use a wide variety of moral languages, such as having a character flaw, not thinking of others, not thinking of consequences, or practicing bad judgment. These different moral languages arise from the multiple ways in which the general revelation of God's moral law is received into human consciousness.

God's common grace is his call to repentance.

At the point in the text which we call "chapter 2," Paul transitions from teaching missionaries (and therefore all Christians) how to *think about* people who are without the gospel to demonstrating how he *preaches to* people who are without the biblical message. He shifts from speaking in the third person ("they" and "them") to the second person ("you"). But the people he is addressing as "you" are probably not the initial readers of this epistle in the church at Rome. They are a hypothetical "you," meaning their neighbors in the Greco-Roman world who need the gospel. They represent our neighbors around the globe or next door.

Most of the initial readers of this letter to the church in Rome had never heard Paul preach to the unbelieving world, and the texts we call Acts 14:8-18 and Acts 17:16-34, where we have a record of how Paul preached to the people in the Gentile world, had not yet been written. The missionaries in training, the members of the church in Rome, needed some type of input, whether as a role model or as general principles, about how to connect the gospel which they believed with the lives and experience of their neighbors. Paul shifts to saying "you" to give a generalized example or role model of how Christian missionaries should connect the gospel to the moral/spiritual life of the people to whom they are bringing their witness.

We can read verses 2:1-5 as the outline of a sermon, lecture, or private discussion, the content of which could also be explained at great length. The content of these verses is pre-evangelistic, meaning it is designed to lead up to explaining the gospel about salvation by faith in Christ at a later time. Paul's presentation in this paragraph assumes the previously described deep contradictions within human experience and the conflict of every person with God, but then Paul takes his discussion partners a step farther. There are at least two conclusions Paul wants his hearers or discussion partners to reach, either of which can prompt people to recognize they need forgiveness in Christ:

1. that the suppressed knowledge that they deserve the wrath of God stands in tension with their experience of God's common grace, so they know they receive better than they deserve;
2. that they acknowledge that they know and use the natural moral law in evaluating their neighbors but refuse to use the natural moral law to point out their own sin, showing that their internal

moral/spiritual life is knowingly a defense against important truths they suppress.

Though some of Paul's hypothetical hearers or discussion partners may conclude that they are already experiencing God's wrath in the form of being given over to sin, other hypothetical hearers may conclude they deserve wrath even though they have received undeserved common grace. Either of these conclusions, when reached, can begin the decisive change of mind (repentance) which has to accompany faith in the gospel. Though the wrath of God by which he lets people go in their sin can be observed, people should also sense or observe that they receive less of God's wrath than they deserve. The goodness, kindness, and generosity in the universe and in society come from God, and even prior to the gospel, people should recognize that this kindness comes from God. As Paul preached in Lystra, God "has not left himself without testimony. He has shown kindness by giving you rain from heaven and crops in their seasons; he provides you with plenty of food and fills your hearts with joy." (Acts 14:17) All good gifts come from God, and everyone would recognize openly that all good gifts come from God, were they not suppressing God's general revelation. In a very important sense, people already know that they receive good gifts from God, though they may not be able to admit to themselves that they know this to be true.

This common generosity of God calls for both gratitude and a "change of mind." (See 2:4.) Those who have read the Sermon on the Mount (Matthew 5-7) will hear an echo of the words of Jesus, "But I tell you, love your enemies and pray for those who persecute you, that you may be children of your Father in heaven. He causes his sun to rise on the evil and the good, and sends rain on the righteous and the unrighteous." (Matthew 5:44, 45) Whether or not a person knows the words of Jesus, he/she should be aware of being one of the unrighteous to whom God still sends the sun and the rain, but that awareness may need to be brought back into consciousness in pre-evangelistic discussion with a Christian.

In Romans 2:4 Paul uses four complementary words to describe the riches of God's common grace, using one more descriptor than he used when he said God "gave them over." It may not be possible to precisely define the exact differences among these four words in Paul's Greek, but that is probably not the point of using four words. Rather, the extravagance of the description of God's everyday common grace, in light of the preceding description of God's wrath, is already a hint that grace can overcome wrath.

It is noteworthy that Paul does not in any way mention forgiveness of sin in relation to God's common grace. God's forbearance, by which God practices kindness when more wrath is deserved, is, at most, an indication that forgiveness may be possible. Paul does not mention true forgiveness of sin until he talks about the gospel. His description of God's common grace prepares people to also repent and believe in the gospel of forgiveness by faith in Jesus. Reminding people of God's common grace, helping them to unrepress their knowledge of God's common grace, is a crucial step that prepares people to hear the gospel that Jesus died and rose in order to provide special, saving grace.

Short Definitions
1. Common grace is the undeserved kindness of God whereby he sends rain on the just and the unjust and also gives us all the other gifts that make life possible. People from many religions and philosophies of life acknowledge that what we receive is a gift from above but usually without saying that this grace is a call to repentance.
2. Special grace is the undeserved kindness of God related to the gospel of salvation in Christ. We learn about and receive this grace through the message of the Bible and the related means God has given us, such as preaching, sacraments, prayer, and fellowship. Forgiveness of sin is central in special grace.

To bring about the kind of spiritual self-awareness that is a change of mind, Paul demonstrates how to help people consider their own moral/cultural experience in a manner that tends to "unrepress" knowledge that has previously been repressed into the subconscious. (See verses 2:1-3.) He starts with the observation that we are all evaluating the actions of everyone around us, and we all know that everyone else is evaluating us. We can see the sins and shortcomings of the people around us, even if we are too polite to say much about it. And we know that everyone around us can see many of our sins and weaknesses, even if they are too polite to say much about our sins. The normal human experience is that we condemn others for sins they commit, even though we expect to escape God's condemnation for committing similar sins ourselves. This is obviously illogical. And this standard illogical jump, observable all over the world, illustrates our suppressed knowledge of God's law and wrath! Paul's pre-evangelistic discussion helps people to acknowledge those truths they prefer not to acknowledge but which they must acknowledge if they are to come to real faith.

Paul assumes, if we are not psychopaths, that we all know that other people are constantly evaluating our actions in this manner. There is continuous social pressure, whether hidden or open, to make our outward actions conform to a socially accepted set of rules, so that others will not evaluate or judge us too severely. This total process of evaluating each other (and being aware of the process of mutual moral evaluation) has a huge benefit: much of the time it makes life in society possible, so that we behave like civilized humans according to the standards of some civilization, not like wild beasts. And in many people who become truly good people, according to the standards of a society, profession, family, or role, this process of evaluation becomes truly internalized, so that people truly want to be "good" within their roles and situation, whether as good family members, good citizens, good role models, or good professionals. It is one of the means of God's common grace which partly restrains people from fully following all their sinful tendencies, while they also practice many moral virtues which correspond with God's natural moral law; this total process is part of the basis for every culture.

Because this process assumes a vague but significant knowledge of God's natural moral law, older writers on Christian ethics used to talk about the "civil use of God's law" in this regard. But regardless of which culture a person inhabits, whether more collectivist or individualist, whether more shame-oriented or more guilt-oriented, inside the person there is this terribly illogical process of condemning others when we expect to escape condemnation for the same actions. Jesus warned about judging others precisely because we are all doing it all the time in order to make ourselves look good in our own eyes and avoid having to think about God's demands and wrath.

Paul's method of discussion bears a distinct resemblance to the method reportedly used in ancient Greece by Socrates and Plato. They used questions and dialogue to help people clarify what they thought and knew, and often to discover that people knew truths they were not aware of knowing. Even though it is portrayed so briefly, Paul's method of dialogue goes much deeper than did that of Socrates or Plato, to consider the wrath and grace of God, not merely the unchanging principles and sources of knowledge which Plato brought to mind. Plato might use the "Socratic method" to demonstrate that even the simplest person knows what a perfect circle is, even though no one has ever seen a truly perfect circle. Paul's missionary method of discussion takes an ultimate step deeper than Plato, to the truly overwhelming consideration that even the person who claims to be an atheist or a polytheist knows much about God's wrath and common grace. When he says, "… we know that the judgment of God is based on truth when it falls on those who take such inappropriate actions …" (2:2), the "we" is probably all people, not only believers. He writes "we know" in the sense that all people know, hold down, and suppress these truths, while these suppressed truths also form the moral condition of normal human experience.

The suppression of knowledge leaves people with constant cognitive dissonance, the condition of holding two contradictory beliefs or opinions. Conflict with God is the basis for this cognitive dissonance, which forms Paul's starting point for his preaching. He both explains the dissonance (by his explanation of normal human experience) and offers the solution, peace with God by faith in the gospel of Jesus.

> Jesus' statement, "Do not judge or you too will be judged" (Matthew 7:1), is well- known and uses the same Greek terminology which Paul uses in Romans 2:1. Both Jesus and Paul assume that mutual judging or evaluating is common in all societies, because people are both sinful and aware of a moral standard. The point of Jesus' command seems to be that we must stop putting ourselves in the place of God, as if we are the judge of others, that we must stop assuming we are morally superior to others (who only have a speck of dust in their eyes compared with the wooden plank in our eyes), and that we must stop thinking that God will not hold us accountable, if we happen to be able to excuse ourselves from our sins. Paul takes

> the teaching of Jesus and applies it globally as a starting point for world missions, connecting Jesus' teaching with Paul's understanding of how God's general revelation and common grace work in life and society.

The Solution: Thoughtful Pride in the Gospel

The people to whom we have to bring the gospel of Christ are already wrestling with God's general revelation. Though it is repressed, so that they are not always fully aware of it, our neighbors know a lot about God. What they know from God forms the foundation for daily life and makes society possible, even though this knowledge may be rejected. As part of their conflict with God, people are now experiencing God's temporal wrath and probably even know they are experiencing God's wrath, while at the same time people receive better than they deserve from God and probably know that they receive better than they deserve from God. People are constantly using God's natural moral law to evaluate each other, while, in a totally irrational manner, people hope to excuse themselves on the basis of this same moral law.

Paul's understanding of the human condition before God forms the background and foundation for his short outline of themes for a pre-evangelistic dialogue with people who need the gospel. We can learn to talk with our neighbors about these themes as well. Paul's mission work assumed that the people to whom he was speaking already had a long history of conflict with the God whom they knew, whose law they knew, needed, used, and alternately liked or disliked, but whom they pretended not to know. They were experiencing both God's wrath and his common grace. This understanding made Paul unashamed of the gospel. He was proud of the gospel, and this pride in the gospel was central for being prepared for his mission work.

The gospel is the message that God has not left the human race in the predicament we have made for ourselves. It is the message of forgiveness and reconciliation with God, the end of conflict with God, leading to the beginning of a new way of life that is marked by a renewed heart and mind, replacing the darkened heart and mind. This new way of life is in closer conformity with the law of God and the scheme of nature, and for this reason it is also much more honorable.

Paul's assessment of the human condition before God has obvious deep roots in the Old Testament. In addition to being a commentary on the early chapters of Genesis and picking up themes from Isaiah, it also appropriates the claim of the prophets, that the human problem is not primarily that people do not know right and wrong but that people do not want to follow the knowledge of right and wrong that has been given by God to all people. Paul expects that his readers will be able to see that thoughtful people should be ashamed of and embarrassed by their many substitute religions, and therefore Christians can become unashamed of the Christian gospel. And as a role model in missionary dialogue, Paul shows believers how to lead unbelievers through their moral experience to perceive their repressed knowledge of God's wrath and common grace; this perception is the change of mind, the repentance that accompanies faith in the gospel.

A person on the way to faith in the gospel should accept Paul's message because it simultaneously allows a person to understand and also to accept his/her previously rejected knowledge of God and all of God's general revelation. The biblical message allows us to understand human experience, including both our own personal experience and also the moral experience of life in society. The biblical message presents a promise in which we must trust (the gospel), but before presenting the gospel, the biblical message explains the conditions that have to be true if we are to understand everything else, especially ourselves and the unbelief of our neighbors. And at the center of our certainty and confidence is the experience of being called to the Father through the gospel of Jesus, instead of being "given over" to self-destruction in his wrath.

There is a solution to the human condition. The gospel of Jesus Christ is worthy of proclamation! We can be unashamed.

Interlude on contemporary theology: representative distortions from the twentieth century that Christians must avoid in the twenty first century

In the first sections of this study we have engaged in a targeted exposition and application of selected themes from Romans 1:16-2:5 which elucidate the description of the condition of the human race as "wrestling with God's general revelation." There is no other option for people who do not know the gospel of Christ; God's general revelation is truly central, honestly essential, to all of human experience, even though much of the human race is investing their time and energy into pushing their awareness of all the contents of God's general revelation out of consciousness. This is the divine-human wrestling match that has continued throughout all of history since the fall into sin. But we are not the first Christians to think about and describe God's general revelation. Much of what previous generations of Christians have said about God's general revelation has been very good and has been included into our exposition of this theme from Romans. But in the 2,000 years of Christian history there have been various distorted directions related to thinking about and responding to God's general revelation.

We will briefly examine three representative distortions from the twentieth century which are very different from each other and which illustrate the range of problems which can be expected to recur among Christians in the twenty first century. Many of the other misunderstandings of God's general revelation are similar to one of these three. Two of these distortions were represented by widely respected theologians, Karl Barth (Protestant) and Karl Rahner (Roman Catholic). Obviously the influence of Barth's ideas can be expected more widely among Protestants and Evangelicals, whereas the influence of Rahner's ideas can be expected more commonly among Roman Catholics, but their influence and the ideas they represented can be found far beyond their own churches. A third distortion is represented by a terrible mix of misguided ideas about general revelation with National Socialism and stands as a permanent warning for Christians in regard to political ideologies which combine isolated themes of Christian teaching (separated from other important themes in our faith and ethics) with racism or nationalism.

During the Nazi era in Europe (1933-1945), some Protestant theologians combined a confused theory of general revelation with aspects of the Nazi (National Socialist) ideology and thereby formed the foundation for the "German Christian Movement." While the deeply disturbing details of this movement are beyond our purview, the "German Christians" claimed there was a general revelation of God's law through the law of the "Volk," the Nazi-Germanic people, or, alternately, there was a revelation of God's grace in the work of Adolf Hitler. The different varieties of people and ideas within this movement agreed in claiming there was a revelation from God that came through their people, their nation, or their political party that was not given to other peoples, nations, or parties. Some of these people became the most enthusiastic promoters of National Socialism, saying that supporting Hitler and the Nazis was a duty for Christians or an expression of real Christian faith.[32] When I first read a book by one of these writers, already many years ago, I felt sick and could hardly believe my eyes. I hope your reaction is similar.

Very few Christians today will mix the biblical faith with the German National Socialist ideology from the 1930s and 1940s, but the tragic mistakes of these theologians (and the churches they served) stand as a warning for all time; we must be very careful about how we think about general revelation and its relation to political ideologies and secular worldviews. It was a dreadful mistake to associate the demands of the Nazi state and political party with the real demands of God's natural moral law given to all people through general revelation. It seems to me that they interpreted and appropriated the message of the Bible in light of and on the basis of the Nazi ideology, which both filtered out themes from the Bible and distorted how they understood other themes from the Bible. This theological mistake contributed to the humanitarian disasters of World War II and the Holocaust. Bad theology has astonishingly wide social consequences. If we do not consider the mistakes of the past, we can easily repeat them.

In reaction to the German Christian Movement, Karl Barth (1886-1968), a Swiss Protestant theologian, is properly famous for shouting "Nein!" with such volume that his voice is still echoing in many parts of the church, even when his name is not mentioned.[33] Someone needed to

---

[32] For more on this theme see Robert P. Eriksen, *Theologians Under Hitler: Gerhard Kittel, Paul Althaus, and Emanuel Hirsch* (New Haven and London: Yale University Press, 1985).

[33] One of Barth's influential essays was simply entitled *Nein!*, which means "No!" in German. Barth wrote numerous essays, letters, and books to criticize the Nazis and the "German Christians."

say very loudly and very clearly that the Nazi ideology had to be rejected by Christians as vicious, evil, and contrary to everything that Christians affirm; the heroism of Barth and the other courageous people in the "Confessing Church," which opposed the German Christian Movement, should be noted and imitated. And Barth's rebuke of this terrible distortion should be remembered whenever people are tempted to join faith in Christ with one-sided nationalism or excessive loyalty to any political party or ideology. But Barth's theological explanation of his rejection of the Nazi ideology contained another theological problem. He was concerned that any talk about general revelation tends to reduce the biblical message to be merely a religious dimension of a particular culture, thereby reducing the church to be merely the department of religion of a nation or the religious dimension of a particular society. Too often, he thought, the church has lost the sharp edge of its prophetic criticism of society and secular ideologies and has conformed to the ideas and standards of the secular world. (We must agree with his claim that the church has often lost its prophetic sharp edge and become conformed to the world, without accepting all of his theological explanation of the problem.) He argued vehemently that Christians and the churches must only recognize God's one revelation in Jesus Christ which must be authoritative over all we say, do, and think; even our social and political ethics must be learned entirely from the one revelation in Jesus Christ. This means, according to Barth, that Christians should never discuss general revelation, unless one mentions general revelation only to deny it. On the basis of the one revelation in Christ, and only on this basis, Barth thought Christians can be true critics of all that is evil in society. This rejection of general revelation, saying there is only one revelation from God, the revelation in Jesus Christ, was enshrined in the key Protestant document written in opposition to the German Christian Movement, the *Barmen Confession* of 1934.[34]

We must agree with and enthusiastically applaud Barth's sharp critique of the German Christian Movement and National Socialism, including many of the theological and cultural streams that led up to these movements, but the German Christian Movement suffered from a *misunderstanding* of general revelation; this terribly misguided movement was **not**

---

[34] For more on this theme see Arthur C. Cochrane, *The Church's Confession under Hitler* (Philadelphia: Westminster, 1962) and Robin W. Lovin, *Christian Faith and Public Choices: The Social Ethics of Barth, Brunner, and Bonhoeffer* (Philadelphia: Fortress Press, 1984).

the result of a proper understanding of God's general revelation.[35] The German Christian Movement was idolatry within the circles of the Christian Church. And as we saw in our studies of Romans 1:16-2:5, idolatry is one of the common responses to God's general revelation. A Pauline understanding of general revelation builds on the social criticism of the Old Testament prophets and enables believers and the church to become confident both as critics of society and also as heralds of a gospel that all people need. It was God's general revelation of his moral law that enabled morally sensitive people from many countries (regardless of their faith or lack of faith) to see that National Socialism was evil. There is no reason to follow Barth in his rejection of any discussion of general revelation, as should be evident from our analysis of Romans. The fact that many of the morally sensitive people who resisted National Socialism and the resulting Holocaust were not clear about their own religious convictions can be explained by Paul's claim that God's moral law is known, at least in part, to all people and enables a socially needed process of mutual moral evaluation.[36] Many people knew that National Socialism was wrong and had to be resisted because they used the general revelation of God's natural moral law as a standard of evaluation.[37]

A distorted point of view of the opposite extreme from Karl Barth is found in the writings of a group of Roman Catholic theologians often called "Transcendental Thomists," of whom Karl Rahner (1904-1984) is the most well-known. Whether or not this is completely intended by Rahner, one receives the impression that God's general revelation is so complete that people do not truly need the gospel of Christ which only comes via special revelation. In a manner that implies that special revelation has approximately the same content as general revelation, Rahner wrote, "The

---

[35] Barth claimed that the church and theological movement of "Culture Protestantism" contributed to the cultural conditions which made National Socialism possible. I think Barth was right in this claim, though other cultural streams also contributed to National Socialism. The main varieties of Culture Protestantism rejected the idea of an objective moral law, whether that moral law given in general or special revelation, which left this movement vulnerable to simply conform to sinful movements in society.

[36] For more on this theme, the rejection of general revelation and natural law ethics in twentieth-century Protestant theology, see the appendix.

[37] For an outstanding study of the internal connections between the natural moral law and human rights protections written from the context of resisting totalitarianism, see Pavel Hošek, "The Christian claim for universal human rights in relation to natural law," *International Journal for Religious Freedom*, 5:2, 2012, pp. 147-160.

expressly Christian revelation becomes the explicit statement of the revelation of grace which man always experiences implicitly in the depths of his being."[38] Notice that, in his view, the Christian revelation of grace is the same as the grace which mankind in general experiences.

What we found in Romans 1 and 2 is that people without the gospel should be aware that they receive better than they deserve because of the richness of God's common grace. There is an awareness of common grace available to all people via God' general revelation, though many will suppress this knowledge. But Paul seems to carefully avoid any promise of forgiveness of sins, justification, and the resulting peace with God that is communicated to people by God's common grace and general revelation. Paul's teaching on general revelation and common grace shows the extreme importance of declaring the gospel to all people, a gospel known only by special revelation; Rahner's teaching seems to reduce the importance of declaring the gospel to all people and to reduce the distinction between common grace and special grace.

Rahner is surely right that God's general revelation forms the necessary precondition of human experience, with a result that human life always has a supernatural dimension, a claim which we have noticed in studying Romans 1 and 2. This theme in Rahner's writings provides a needed corrective for all people, whether Christians or not, who talk as if God is not active in the daily life of every person. And I like his elaborate terminology of "the universal supernatural existential," a self-giving presence of God in general revelation which makes and keeps human life human.[39] But Evan-

---

[38] Karl Rahner, *A Rahner Reader,* ed. Gerald A. McCool, (New York: Crossroad, 1981), p. 213. This is from Rahner's essay entitled "Anonymous Christians." I think it is much better not to describe people who claim to be atheists or adherents of other religions as anonymous Christians because a proper respect for people requires that we take their descriptions of themselves very seriously, even if, as I claimed in a previous chapter, many people do not fully believe all the things they say they believe.

[39] I also like Rahner's term "transcendental" which he uses to discuss these questions. Whereas the term "transcendent" usually refers to something independent and separate from the material world, and, therefore, is one of the words we use to describe God, "transcendental" refers to a condition that must exist within the person who knows in order for that person to know something else. In this sense, God's continuous general revelation is the transcendental condition of the normal human experience of knowing. For example, in order for ordinary people, regardless of their faith, to know that murdering a particular person is wrong, they have to know that murder is evil and that people must not do evil. These last areas of knowledge, that murder is evil and that people must not practice evil, are the tran-

gelicals should remind Rahner and his followers that according to the apostle Paul, God holds people accountable, without excuse, and without forgiveness outside of Christ, on the basis of what God has always been speaking and is still speaking through his creation. General revelation, as described in the Bible, is associated with God's law and wrath; God's general revelation, law, and wrath form the framework for understanding and proclaiming the special revelation of the gospel. That special revelation tells us about forgiveness of sins, justification by faith, and peace with God. A proper and serious understanding of God's general revelation will give us missionary courage to confidently and wisely proclaim his special revelation in the Bible and in Jesus Christ.

There have been and will probably continue to be more distorted understandings of God's general revelation within Christian circles. But these three distortions are representative enough that these very brief descriptions can equip thoughtful Christians to perceive other distortions when they appear. In summary, these three distortions are 1. Thinking one's nation or people is a recipient or means of God's revelation in a manner that makes it superior to other nations or peoples; 2. Rejecting the theme of general revelation, as if it were not an essential part of basic Christian teaching; 3. Thinking that God's general revelation makes the special revelation of the gospel of Christ less urgent or even unneeded, with the expectation that people will respond positively to God's general revelation without the special revelation of the gospel. What we have seen from the apostle Paul is that God's general revelation has several areas of content which together provide the conditions which make human life possible; we can continue to live as human beings only because of God's continuing general revelation. But the knowledge of God given through general revelation is constantly suppressed from consciousness because people are hiding from God, even though everyone constantly uses this knowledge for daily life and to evaluate each other and our societies. This rejected knowledge of God can be transformed into the accepted and proper knowledge of God by faith in the gospel of Jesus Christ.

---

scendental conditions of knowing that murdering a particular person is evil. These transcendental conditions are provided by God's general revelation.

Part II: Faith Seeks Understanding

A Missionary Philosophy of the Divine-Human Wrestling Match

In this next part of our study of the way in which the human race is wrestling with God's general revelation we are moving from theology to philosophy. For Christians, theology is broadly the study of knowing God, the gospel, and the application of Scripture to life; this is what we have been doing so far. A worthwhile definition of philosophy, which we will use here, is the analysis of human experience.[40] Philosophical analysis of any topic is usually carried out in light of a person's basic religious or ideological assumptions, which some of our friends call a "ground motive" and others call a "worldview." Because of this normal relation between religion and philosophy, we do not need to make an apology for openly engaging in philosophy in light of understanding the complex conflict that people have with God's general revelation. But the philosophical analysis in which we will now engage has a particular purpose, to help us understand the people to whom God has sent us, as the Body of Christ, as his missionaries.

In the light provided by a Pauline understanding of God's speech through creation, there are many dimensions of human experience that we can begin to understand in their depths. Without thinking in light of God's general revelation, our understanding of these themes will remain superficial. Thinking about human experience in light of general revelation will not only lead to spiritual maturity; it will also prepare believers for the task of taking the gospel to people whose lives are not only shaped by a vast array of religions and philosophies of life, but who also face the whole range of life problems, questions, and deep needs. If, as I believe, we Christians have thought about life in light of general revelation too seldom, this is worth our serious attention. Thinking deeply about human experience in light of the way people are wrestling with God's general revelation will equip us for applying his special revelation and the gospel.

---

[40] If we use these definitions, some parts of the Bible, such as the Old Testament books of Proverbs and Ecclesiastes, contain as much philosophy as theology, showing that the definitions of our terms "theology" and "philosophy" are not extremely precise and that the relation between the two types of study must always remain open.

There are several themes we must consider. The first of these themes is the human experience of Angst. The we will consider the relation of God's general revelation to the human quest, followed by a discussion of how thinking in light of God's general revelation allows us to understand anew how to consider some important questions in religion and philosophy.

Chapter Three: Angst and General Revelation

Summary: In light of God's general revelation, we can understand Angst and its relation to the gospel. Angst arises from the threatening nature of God's general revelation and finds its solution in the multiple dimensions of the gospel.

I have had similar experiences while teaching philosophy in secular universities (where very few of my students claimed to be Christians) and also while preaching in evangelical churches (where most of the people were Christians). When I directly and sensitively take up the topic of Angst, the level of interest has become extraordinarily high, because the people know I am speaking to their real concerns; boredom is banished. In a philosophy class, the students might have a moderate level of interest when comparing different theories that seek to explain how we know, but those students might be sitting on the edge of their chairs, with rapt attention, when I lecture on the question of whether or not life has any meaning. In a church situation, the level of interest may be moderate when talking about when a particular book in the Bible was written or about different theories of what will happen when Jesus returns, but when I preach on anxiety or the emptiness of daily life, everyone is really interested. And when teaching in evangelical theological seminaries, students have expressed the most gratitude when I have offered an outline to describe the varieties of Angst and how the biblical message addresses our Ängste.

So far I have used the words "Angst" and "Ängste" without defining them. We need terminology to describe the human condition of being aware that something is terribly wrong in human life, that we are guilty, fallen, lost in the world, dying, and deserve the wrath of God, even if that awareness might be largely repressed so that it remains preconscious for some individuals. Different terms could be used. For that type of awareness we will select the German word *Angst*, which is generally translated into English as "anxiety" or "dread,"[41] though I do not want to use these Eng-

---

[41] This term has been widely used in European thought, probably first being used in a manner similar to our use in the philosophy of Søren Kierkegaard (1813-1855). He spelled it *angest* in the Danish language. Though this term is somewhat new, probably less than 200 years old, the experience is as old as humanity.

lish words because these words may be too familiar to some and may suggest purely emotional matters to others. The danger in this method of analysis is that some may misunderstand it to be psychology only, instead of an analysis of the entirety of life, including the psychological dimension of life. As used in this context, the word Angst does not refer to a psychological disorder or to the type of problem that might be measured by a psychological anxiety scale or test. We will usually write Angst (Ängste when plural), not anxiety, because it is more comprehensive than psychological disorders in several ways: This is not a disorder of one person or a set of "sick" people in contrast with other "normal" people; it is a condition and set of problems faced by the entire human race, though different people experience it differently. A person may or may not always feel Angst at a psychological or conscious level, since one's awareness of fallenness may be well suppressed, or it may be partly addressed by that person's religion or ideology.

What we are considering is far more than a psychological condition; it is the condition of fallen humanity, of which people are partly conscious, or are conscious with that awareness partly suppressed. For some people, their Angst may be mostly expressed in artistic or philosophical terms, not in psychological traits or disorders, showing that Angst is more than psychological. Some psychological or philosophical discussions of anxiety confuse specific fears (even if called anxieties) with the general human condition of Angst, which may have no conscious object more specific than "life," "problems," or the "world." Personally I find that a cup of green tea may relieve my feelings of anxiety, but it does not eliminate Angst; a cup of tea only gives me a calmer state of mind when I consider the deep issues of meaning, guilt, and uncertainty in my life and in the lives of the people I love. This personal experience illustrates the distinction between the psychological experience of anxiety and the human condition of Angst.

I regret that Paul Tillich used the term *anxiety* to describe what we are calling Angst, though his analysis is very instructive; he defined anxiety as "awareness of possible non-being." In light of our explanation of God's general revelation in the previous chapters, Tillich's definition should be developed and deepened. Let us define Angst as *awareness, often suppressed from consciousness, of our condition as fallen and deserving the wrath of God, which all people have as a result of God's general revelation.* We will distinguish between our objective status as fallen and separated from God and our subjective awareness of our fallen situation; we will use the term Angst to describe our subjective awareness of our fallen condition, not primarily to describe our objective status of fallen and separated from God. Without God's general revelation, we would not be aware or conscious that something is wrong, that we are "by nature" (meaning as a result of sin, not as a result of creation) in conflict with God with effects that disturb all of life. If, after Adam and Eve's sin, God had simply let the human race go its way without him, we would not be aware that something is profoundly wrong in the human condition. But people are often aware that something is not right with the world, and that knowledge is a result of God's continuing general revelation. If we do not recognize that this awareness comes from God's general revelation, it is only because of our sinful habit of suppressing our knowledge of God. Tillich's analysis of anxiety merits our attention as a tool to describe Angst, though one must remember that Tillich saw his study of anxiety as a flexible tool to understand human experience in regard to religious needs, not as an overly rigid diagnostic system.[42]

Following Tillich, there are three major types of Angst, each of which can be experienced on either an ultimate level (in relation to God or a God-substitute) or on a secondary, penultimate level (in relation to ourselves and other people). *Moral* Angst has to do with guilt and fear of condemnation, whether the guilt is in relation to other people, God, or a God-substitute; the fear of ultimate condemnation by God comprises the ultimate form of moral Angst. (If I were to rewrite Tillich's analysis, I would describe the experiences of shame in human relations, rejection by people, and loss of belonging in community as additional varieties of penultimate or secondary moral Angst.)[43] *Existential* Angst has to do with a loss of meaning and purpose. On a secondary level, it is a sense that life is boring, while, on the ultimate level, it is the perception or feeling that life is empty and meaningless, without a guiding purpose and possibly not worth living. *Ontic* Angst (derived from the Greek word *ontos*, referring to all that has being) has to do with our awareness that our entire being is threatened by what will or may happen to us: matters of fate, the future, and death; the

---

[42] As a German immigrant to the US, Tillich (1886-1965) seemed to sometimes think in German while writing in English. For sake of clarity, I am translating his English word "anxiety" back into the German word "Angst." My use of his analysis of anxiety is neither an endorsement of all his opinions nor a recommendation of him as a personal role model. Tillich summarized his analysis of anxiety in *The Courage to Be* (Yale University Press, 1952).

[43] The distinction between guilt and shame has been more sharply clarified by sociologists and anthropologists since the time of Tillich. A good study on the topic is Thomas Schirrmacher, *Culture of Guilt/Culture of Shame,* forthcoming, VKW, Bonn.

fear of death is the ultimate form of ontic Angst. (I will substitute the word "ontological" for Tillich's word "ontic.").

The three types of Angst overlap and mix in the experience of many people, and within the Christian community we tend to mix moral Angst and ontological Angst because of the way in which we describe sin and death. But it is worthwhile to keep the three varieties distinct in our discussion so that we are more equipped to perceive the significant diversity in human experience, even in our consciousness (or repressed awareness) of our fallenness. Tillich thought that our western cultural ancestors in ancient Greece and Rome especially wrestled with ontological anxiety, whereas medieval culture especially had to face moral anxiety, while the European and North American cultures in which he lived during the twentieth century were particularly marked by existential anxiety, the threatening loss of meaning. Broadly, with some exceptions, the inhabitants of a particular historical culture experience the whole range of anxieties as perceived through the lens or filter of one variety of anxiety, so that one variety of Angst plays a leading role in the lives of a group of people.

Religion, Tillich claimed, is the way in which humans find courage to face life in the face of anxiety. People are constantly responding to Angst, seeking salvation and solutions, and the way in which people respond to Angst is their religion. (This is why, as John Calvin observed, "Man's nature is a perpetual factory of idols."[44]) But the forms of Angst and the religious responses to the varieties of Angst display tremendous diversity, depending on the situation of diverse peoples, because cultural diversity influences both our experience of Angst and our religious response. As Tillich noted, perhaps with a bit of exaggeration, "Culture is the form of religion, and religion is the substance of culture."[45] There is a similar relation between culture and Angst, such that both the experience of Angst and the articulation of that Angst vary significantly among cultures as cultures are influenced by the many religions.

If Tillich was right, that each culture has a central Angst through which a group of people experiences the other varieties of Angst, we can and should learn to distinguish the varieties of Angst as part of understanding cultures and the application of the biblical message in different cultures.

---

[44] John Calvin, *Institutes of the Christian Religion*, I.xi.8. Trans. Ford Lewis Battles, ed. John T. McNeill, (Philadelphia, 1960). This version was translated from Calvin's 1559 Latin edition.

[45] Paul Tillich, *Theology of Culture* (Oxford University Press, 1959), p. 42. There is probably a bit of conscious exaggeration in this slogan, since some commonalities among all cultures flow from our common humanity, created in the image of God.

We can also notice the way in which the varieties of Angst gain additional power in human experience because of the ways in which they overlap and penetrate each other. Based merely on my personal observations of students and neighbors, I have the impression that many Europeans experience existential Angst as primary and perceive the other Ängste through the lens of a loss of meaning, whereas many North Americans today experience moral Angst as primary and frequently experience the other Ängste through the lens of guilt or forgiveness.

The analysis of Angst can be used within evangelical missions, preaching, and pastoral care if we understand it within the framework Paul gives us in Romans 1:16-2:5. Angst, in all its varieties, is ultimately the result of the threatening and condemning character of God's general revelation, though there are also secondary causes for Angst which lead to its multicolored rainbow texture. Were God's general revelation to cease, our Ängste would also be laid to rest, but the cost would be the loss of our humanity, reducing us to be mere brutes. As far as I can observe, my dog does not experience Angst, though I think he is sometimes lonely or depressed. At the beginning God created us by speaking us into existence, and he did so by means of speaking to us in a manner that was different from the way in which he spoke the rest of creation into existence. He created us to respond to him consciously, in his image, whereas the rest of creation responds to God's creating word without the same type of consciousness. God maintains our humanness by continuing to speak the same word to us which he spoke in creation, which we now call his general revelation. This creating word of God made us human and keeps us human today, but in our fallenness, it also continually keeps us partly aware of our fallen condition with a kind of knowledge which I call Angst.

Of course Angst is often unpleasant, but the unpleasantness of Angst should not blind us from seeing how it is associated with both God's common grace and his special, saving grace. God's general revelation, by which he gives his common grace, necessarily and continuously causes a reaction in fallen, sinful humans. And that human reaction of Angst is part of our continuing preparation for the good news of redemption in Christ. As the ultimate background for all human Angst, we must remember Paul's claim that people "know the requirement of God that those who do such things are worthy of death" (Romans 1:32), which he mentions in order to both explain why people need the gospel and to prepare believers to proclaim the gospel courageously.

Far from neglecting Angst and spiritual need, the biblical message both brings the full range of Ängste to articulate expression (A few of the psalms are quoted below as an example.) and then applies the promises of God's grace and the gospel, leading to hope, comfort, joy, and courage. As Christians we grasp the importance and beauty of the biblical message when we openly connect its promises and narratives to our experience of Angst. This normal Christian experience provides a key for talking about the gospel with our neighbors. We should frequently mention the normal human experiences of guilt, shame, lack of purpose, inner emptiness, and fear of the future when we talk about Jesus, so that people perceive more quickly that the biblical message connects with their spiritual needs. If we do not mention this connection, it is more likely that people will interpret our account of the birth, death, and resurrection of Jesus as an ancient fairy tale that is irrelevant today.

Angst does not necessarily end the moment we come to faith. Though there is diversity of experience among believers, it is very common that we repeatedly or even continually move from the condition of Angst to the assurance arising from faith, and, vice versa, from the assurance arising from faith back to a condition of Angst. Our entire existence in all its dimensions is continually threatened by fate, guilt, and emptiness, so that authentic faith always has to be newly reaffirmed as we repeatedly reaffirm our trust in the promises of God.[46]

Many psalms begin with a heart-rending expression of Angst expressed in prayer to God, often leading to renewed trust in God and peace with life. A few examples must suffice, though it is important for people both inside and outside the church to be familiar with this theme so that all know that faith is a response to Angst, not a denial of Angst.

Psalm 3: Lord, how many are my foes! How many rise up against me! Many are saying of me, "God will not deliver him."

Psalm 4: Answer me when I call to you, my righteous God. Give me relief from my distress; have mercy on me and hear my prayer.

Psalm 5: Listen to my words, Lord, consider my lament. Hear my cry for help, my King and my God, for to you I pray.

Psalm 6: Lord, do not rebuke me in your anger or discipline me in your wrath. Have mercy on me, Lord, for I am faint; heal me, Lord, for my bones are in agony. My soul is in deep anguish. How long, Lord, how long?

---

[46] Some of the most central continuing themes of the Christian life are encapsulated in the title of the hymn "Trust and Obey," written by John H. Sammis in 1887. In light of ever-new situations (which easily cause Angst), we must trust God's promises and obey his commands. Both trust and obedience are new every day.

Chapter Three: Angst and General Revelation

> Psalm 10: Why, Lord, do you stand far off? Why do you hide yourself in times of trouble?
>
> Psalm 13: How long, Lord? Will you forget me forever? How long will you hide your face from me? How long must I wrestle with my thoughts and day after day have sorrow in my heart?
>
> Psalm 22: My God, my God, why have you forsaken me? Why are you so far from saving me, so far from my cries of anguish?

Everyone comes to the Bible with his or her distinct experiences of Angst which shape all that he or she reads and hears. Therefore, we have to be careful about how our experiences of the varieties of Angst and our interpretations of Angst influence what we see and find in the Bible. One of the reasons why Christians in different eras have thought they read slightly different messages in the Bible is that they have come to the Bible with different expectations. These different expectations are shaped by different experiences of Angst and different interpretations of our Ängste. I believe that the Bible contains an objective message which reflects God's intentions, but there is an inevitable subjective element in the application of the Bible because of the wide range of expectations and Ängste that we bring to the Bible. The solution, which brings us closer to God's intentions, is to read the Bible very carefully, attempting to allow the Bible to reformat our own spiritual needs. And it is very helpful for us to learn how Christians living in other times and places read and understand the biblical message; when others understand and apply the Bible in light of expectations different from our own, we often see the weaknesses in the expectations we have brought to the Bible.

Just as we inevitably read the Bible in light of our own experience of Angst, we should also attempt to "read" or interpret our neighbors' experience of Angst in light of the biblical message. This is part of the work which students of missions call "contextualizing" the gospel or which we can call missionary philosophy.

During the process of coming to faith in Christ (as well as during the whole Christian life), the Holy Spirit makes use of the internal correlations between human Ängste and the biblical message both to apply the gospel to our needs and to confirm the truthfulness of the biblical message to our consciousness. Most of the many millions of Christians in the last 2,000 years did not have access to sophisticated books that used the theoretical methods of their eras to "prove" the truth of the gospel according to the cultural standards and definitions of truth used in those many eras.[47] Yet many millions have known with confidence that the gospel is true. The truth and importance of the gospel have been recognized by normal believers through the centuries because the Holy Spirit gives the direct intuition that the Voice which speaks of redemption, forgiveness, and peace with God in Jesus (special revelation) is the same Voice which echoes through the entire universe (general revelation) that people are "worthy of death." (Romans 1:32) Therefore, we should consider the profound way in which the biblical message both explains Angst (arising from our confrontation with God's general revelation) and applies redemption to the deepest human needs.[48] Much of the certainty of faith arises from this correlation.

> Note for students of theology and humanities: In this and following sections, I am using what theologians call a "method of correlation," which means correlating (or connecting at the deepest level) the Ängste, questions, and needs found in human existence with the answers and solutions found in the biblical revelation, assuming there is variety in how different people and cultures experience and interpret those needs and questions. This correlation exists and can be discussed because God is the author of both general revelation (including the moral law), which brings awareness of Ängste and questions, and special revelation (centered in the gospel), which brings solutions and answers. In the twentieth century the term "method of correlation" was heavily used by Paul Tillich, who is not usually seen as a role model for evangelicals, but the method itself is much older and was clearly used already by Martin Luther (1483-1546), the key founder of the Reformation movement. (See Wayne G. Johnson, *Theological Method in Luther and Tillich: Law, Gospel, and Correlation,* University Press of America, 1983.) What we call a method of correlation today is only a development in terminology from the relationship between law and

---

[47] God's definition of truth, which is the only truly objective definition of truth, is without doubt, different from the definitions of truth found in some of our cultures.

[48] What I am recommending should not be confused with what is sometimes called "felt-needs preaching." The "needs" that people feel may be desires that are sinful ("I need heroin.") or the result of false religious assumptions ("I need wealth to be happy."), and people do not always feel their real Angst, since awareness of Angst may be repressed. Talking about the varieties of Angst can unrepress a person's awareness of his real situation, so that he begins to feel needs that were previously repressed from consciousness. The entire Bible is God's response to human spiritual needs, though people do not always feel those needs.

gospel, which has been central for evangelical theology and ethics since Luther's time.

The way I am using the method of correlation is heavily influenced by Helmut Thielicke (1908-1986), who emphasized that it is the job of Christian theologians and pastors to articulate and clarify the questions and needs within human experience as a step toward preaching the gospel, though Thielicke did not so closely connect Angst with God's general revelation. (See Helmut Thielicke, *The Evangelical Faith* (3 vols.), Vol. 1, *Prolegomena: The Relation of Theology to Modern Thought Forms*, trans. and ed. by G. W. Bromiley, Eerdmans, 1974.) One of the most popular uses of the method of correlation in Christian literature is found in the Heidelberg Catechism (1563), in which the entire Christian faith is explained in answer to a most fundamental human question, "What is your only comfort, in life and in death?", where the authors clearly assume that the need for comfort represents the entirety of the range of human Ängste and needs, such as hope and courage. The method this catechism uses for basic Christian teaching must also be used in our entire mission work.

Correlation is one of several relations of the biblical message to human experience and cultures. Other relations include critique, construction, and contribution, each of which flows from one of the multiple uses of God's moral law, keeping the relation between law and gospel central in our minds. Such a multifaceted application of the Bible to cultures is a key to a proper contextualization of the Bible that does not risk a loss of Christian identity or truth claims and leads to a proper holism and spiritual balance.

Chapter Four: Moral Angst

When God first spoke to Adam and Eve after the Fall, our first parents were quick to justify themselves, Adam blaming Eve, while Eve blamed the serpent. Neither quickly cried out, "God, be merciful to me, a sinner." They attempted to cover their true guilt before God by means of assigning false guilt to each other, while also covering their shame with tree leaves. As true sons and daughters of Adam and Eve, ever since that time, we have been engaged in a similar process: A primordial awareness of ultimate guilt that deserves condemnation leads to a range of secondary symptoms of moral Angst, whether declaring ourselves just and able to do whatever is required of us, implementing a vast range of attempts to cover our shame (sometimes as silly as Adam and Eve) or assigning false guilt to each other (or even to ourselves). In his moral philosophy, Immanuel Kant (1724-1804) famously argued, "You can because you ought."[49] With these words he was not only representing the best of secular western thought; he was also representing sinful man, vainly attempting to suppress his awareness of real guilt that deserves condemnation before God. Movies, television shows, novels, art, and poetry are filled with the themes of duty, condemnation, guilt, shame, acceptance/rejection, and false guilt. These are central themes of moral-Angst-filled humanity; these themes fill our lives, our dreams, and our relationships.

There is a range of typical reactions of people to moral Angst:
1. They try to reduce what they think God demands to a manageable minimum so they can meet the demands.
2. They claim they can do whatever is required of them.
3. They develop a system of self-cleansing or sacrifice, whether as a part of an organized religion or as a compulsive personal habit.
4. They may deny the existence of God.
5. They may deny the existence of a real moral law, which we call moral relativism.
6. They deny or radically minimize their sinfulness.

---

[49] This is one of the ethical principles that Kant argued in his *Metaphysics of Morals* (originally published in 1797 in German as *Die Metaphysik der Sitten*). It is sometimes rephrased "Ought implies can," and is taken as representative of important themes in the European Enlightenment. To be fair to Kant, we must mention that he also talked about "Radical Evil," a theme which others forget.

7. They develop an array of therapies and techniques to help them feel good about themselves or to accept themselves, a theme in many types of self-help psychology.
8. They may deny the existence of a real self that deserves condemnation, seen in types of Buddhism and some western philosophy.
9. They may say that all guilt is false guilt, that no true moral guilt exists.
10. They may claim that shame is only related to a particular culture and not related to their ultimate moral condition.

The real solution to moral Angst begins with a prayer something like that of David: "Have mercy on me, O God, according to your unfailing love; according to your great compassion blot out my transgressions." (Psalm 51:1) But David knew that God's love was unfailing and that his transgressions could be blotted out only because he knew God's historical revelation to Israel. From that source David learned that God had really forgiven real sinners, such as Abraham, Isaac, and Jacob. From that source David had learned about the whole system of sacrifices of animals. The answer to David's moral Angst was communicated historically, not through God's general revelation, showing us something crucial about the relation between Angst and history. Angst is a universal human condition, shaping all of humanity, while people can generally only look for solutions from those religious options which are available in their historical situation. (Globalization allows people to have contact with a wider range of religious solutions to be found in various cultures.) This is why there is very commonly a question/answer relation between Angst and history. The real solution, which David knew partly but truly, is the gospel of Jesus Christ, of which Paul was so proud. The real solution to moral Angst is that believers "are justified freely by his grace through the redemption that came by Christ Jesus. God presented him as a sacrifice of atonement through faith in his blood." (Romans 3:23, 24)

Without this solution, non-Christian religions, worldviews, and philosophies strongly tend to preach works righteousness and self-salvation, though some promote faith in a Christ substitute. Salvation by God's grace in Christ is the only real solution to moral Angst; at the same time, it directly contradicts many natural ideas of our sinful hearts which are inappropriate responses to moral Angst. The Bible preaches salvation by grace alone, while our sinful hearts, knowing in a repressed manner that we are worthy of condemnation for our sins, preach some variety of salvation by means of human effort.[50] Even after we have been Christians for many years, in the moment of moral Angst, the sinful nature sometimes whispers in our ears, "You do not really need God's forgiveness and grace. You can do all he demands." This whisper, if we believe it, either drives us to proud self-confidence or into despair.

We can grasp a significant self-contradiction in modern culture if we think of it in light of moral Angst. On the one hand, modern culture has been saying for several generations that there is no Original Sin. Whether you read a children's schoolbook, a newspaper, or a philosophical text, everyone seems to agree that human problems are in our environment or society, that there is no problem within the human heart, at the core of our being. Curiously, citizens of the western democracies are likely to agree with Karl Marx in denying the reality of Original Sin. On the other hand, Original Sin is the Christian doctrine that seems to be most easily proved empirically. It is far easier to prove the reality of Original Sin, or at least to provide significant documentation, than it is to prove the Resurrection of Jesus. To prove the Resurrection takes detailed historical work. To prove Original Sin, at least in the sense of illustration, we only need to turn on the television, read a newspaper, or glance at an internet news service. The main way the news differs from one day to the next is who is killing whom and then claiming to be doing a good thing by killing him. Almost every page of every news report verifies the fact that moral Angst is not without reason; we are truly guilty, even while modern culture seems united in preaching the goodness of man.[51]

The explanation of this contradiction, between denying our sinfulness even though our sin is so easy to document, is that the sinful heart is constantly trying to justify itself before the accusing law coming from God's general revelation. This self-justification requires a suppression of God's general revelation. We need to understand Romans 1:32, "They know the requirement of God that those who do such things are worthy of death," in order to understand this important religious dynamic inside people and cultures. Understanding moral Angst is important for gospel proclamation, education, and pastoral care.

When we talk with our neighbors about Jesus, they may not know our Christian terminology about sin, and they may not know the biblical account of Adam and Eve, but they very commonly have the experience of

---

[50] Salvation by human effort is sometimes the effort of an individual and sometimes the effort of a collective. I see Communism as an example of an attempt to earn salvation by means of the efforts of a collective, the proletariat.

[51] No parent has ever had to teach children how to do bad things.

moral Angst. People experience guilt, shame, and fear of condemnation, even if they claim to be atheists or adherents of another religion. And many sense that they receive better than they deserve (awareness of God's common grace). Moral Angst is one of the first themes I notice when I watch a movie or an entertainment program on TV or listen to popular music. Some of this experience of moral Angst will be in relation to other people and to human communities, and some of this experience of moral Angst will mostly be in relation to the universe and to God. As messengers of the gospel, we should display courage and gentleness because we know why people have the experience of moral Angst (conflict with God's general revelation, the ever continuing divine-human wrestling match), while we also offer the only real solution, forgiveness by faith in Jesus. One of the first questions we must ask people who are considering the Christian message is why they experience guilt, shame, and the fear of rejection and condemnation; then we must ask what they think the solution is, and if the solution to Angst offered by their historical/cultural tradition is sufficient. Then the stage is set for the gospel.

Chapter Five: Existential Angst

Not everyone dares to agree with Albert Camus, but thoughts and feelings similar to his plague the minds of many: "There is but one serious philosophical problem, and that is suicide. Judging whether life is or is not worth living amounts to answering the fundamental question of philosophy."[52] Against Camus, some people have argued that the question of the meaning or purpose of life is itself a meaningless question, not worthy of serious consideration or discussion; others maintain that there are only meanings of particular objects, events, and practices within particular cultures, so that no general meaning of life or the universe can exist. But the representatives of both these views protest too loudly! Do the questions Camus raised cause so much anxiety that some feel compelled to close the door on the topic, to suppress the questions?

When lecturing on Camus in universities, I have always told my students that Camus did not recommend suicide; so please do not kill yourself, even if his question raises the deepest levels of Angst. At the very least, Camus recommended that people continue with life as a protest against the absurdity of a life that seems so meaningless. Obviously I think there is a better answer to the lack of meaning, an answer found in the Bible, and there are indications that Camus came to similar conclusions by the end of his life.[53] As a part of training for the mission God has given us, we can begin to talk about the entire Bible as the answer to existential Angst and the loss of meaning, so that in certain contexts our whole mission as Christians can be described as a response to the emptiness of life experienced by people without the gospel. I interpret the experience of meaninglessness, existential Angst, as part of separation from God, while the question about the meaning of life is, I believe, a question that God asks through his general revelation as a means of driving us to see our need for the gospel. This merits explanation.

The great atheist philosopher of the last century, Bertrand Russell, honestly articulated the problem of meaning, if God does not exist. His words merit our meditation.

---

[52] These are the opening lines of "The Myth of Sisyphus," one of Albert Camus's classic essays.
[53] Some of Camus's personal story is told by Howard Mumma, *Albert Camus and the Minister* (Brewster, Massachusetts: Paraclete Press, 2000).

"That Man is the product of causes which had no prevision of the end they were achieving; that his growth, his hopes and fears, his loves and his beliefs, are but the outcome of accidental collocations of atoms; that no fire, no heroism, no intensity of thought and feeling, can preserve an individual life beyond the grave; that all the labors of the ages, all the devotion, all the inspiration, all the noonday brightness of human genius, are destined to extinction in the vast death of the solar system, and that the whole temple of human achievement must inevitably be buried beneath the debris of a universe in ruins—all these things, if not quite beyond dispute, are yet so nearly certain, that no philosophy which rejects them can hope to stand. Only within the scaffolding of these truths, only on the firm foundation of unyielding despair, can the soul's habitation be safely built."[54]

In response to Russell, my teacher George Forell commented, "Here is an honest man speaking. This is what he honestly believes ... Whenever people have contemplated the human condition in ruthless honesty, they have despaired ... Because of their revolt against God, human beings are separated from the one source of meaning and eventually overwhelmed by meaninglessness."[55]

Russell's words are the reflections of a son of Adam who has not only been expelled from the Garden of Eden but also cannot find a way back; both the Garden and the Creator have disappeared from his sight, so he supposes that he himself, with all his hopes, fears, and loves, is merely a fascinating cosmic accident, even while other dimensions of his mind and soul remind him of something else. With terrible irony, as an atheist, he can hardly describe the human race without accidentally referring back to the Garden of Eden. His despair of meaning was, I believe, an experience of separation from God which was also God's call to change his mind and embrace a real answer to meaning in life. If human beings are only "the outcome of accidental collocations of atoms," why would we even ponder the meaning of life?

The Bible provides an analysis of meaning and despair that is surprisingly similar to that of Camus and Russell; the question becomes painfully sharp in the wisdom literature of the Old Testament. "'Meaningless! Meaningless!' says the Teacher. 'Utterly meaningless! Everything is meaningless.' What does man gain from all his labor at which he toils under the

---

[54] Bertrand Russell, *Selected Papers of Bertrand Russell* (New York: Random House, 1927) pp. 2, 3, as quoted by George W. Forell, *The Protestant Faith* (Philadelphia: Fortress Press, 1975), pp. 145, 146.

[55] Forell, p. 146.

sun? Generations come and generations go, but the earth remains forever." (Ecclesiastes 1:2, 3)

Unavoidable facts drive the biblical philosopher to despair: the endless repetition of human life, the endless repetition of events in the natural world, and the expectation that we will both die and then be forgotten by later generations. He engages this type of Angst, painfully probing a deep wound in the human soul, even if the anxiety produced by the questions seems overwhelming. It was by costly experience that the writer of Ecclesiastes discovered that wealth, pleasure, parties, work, and accomplishments did not provide sufficient meaning; outward success could be accompanied by such deep inward emptiness that he was driven to screaming on paper. Pause and think: generations of people, billions of people, have lived and died in an uncaring world that simply keeps spinning through the universe; like those who came before, we will die and be forgotten forever. At best, for those with jobs, we have the endless repetition of going to work and coming home again, day after day after day. I really understand why many people try to forget themselves by means of endless entertainment, drugs, and alcohol, avoiding the thought that it may all be empty.

As Ecclesiastes wrestles with the loss of meaning, he also discovers for us why we wrestle with the question of meaning: God "has set eternity in the hearts of men." (Ecclesiastes 3:11) The anguished cry for ultimate meaning is a part of creation and replies to God's voice echoing through the universe. It is really God who is asking us if our lives have any meaning. Therefore, to find meaning on an ultimate level, he has to find meaning in relation to God. He concludes his study of existential Angst, "Now all has been heard; here is the conclusion of the matter. Fear God and keep his commandments, for this is the whole duty [or meaning] of man." (Ecclesiastes 12:13) But, we must carefully notice, in addition to ultimate meaning, Ecclesiastes also finds multiple secondary or penultimate meanings. These include enjoying the God-given gifts of food, drink, work (2:24-26), and marriage (9:7-9), as well as the general life of wisdom recommended throughout the book. (e.g., 9:13-11:6)

"Go, eat your food with gladness, and drink your wine with a joyful heart, for it is now that God favors what you do. Always be clothed in white, and always anoint your head with oil. Enjoy life with your wife, whom you love, all the days of this meaningless life that God has given you under the sun—all your meaningless days. For this is your lot in life and in your toilsome labor under the sun." (Ecclesiastes 9:7-9)

In these words the author still considers the meaninglessness of life under the sun, but the bitter anguish he has expressed in earlier paragraphs is now gone. Once God is in the picture, he is no longer searching for ultimate meaning in the everyday realm of food, drink, work, and love. He is free to enjoy life, even when it seems empty for a moment, because he is beginning to find ultimate meaning in relation to God.

The relation between ultimate meaning (in relation to God) and secondary meanings (in relation to creation) provides the clue to understanding important themes in our lives (and our neighbors' lives) that seem to be on the border between the ultimate and the secondary. Think about important values such as love, justice, mercy, honesty, loyalty, and patience. A moment's reflection on our own experience will show that we feel a duty to practice these values in relation to other people; we also know that one of our deepest needs is for others around us to practice these values in relation to us; and further, we experience meaning or fulfillment when we practice these values in our work, our family, our communities, and all our relationships. An atheist could say that these are simply interesting psychological observations, but as a Christian, I see God's general revelation of his moral attributes, which gives us a key to understanding meaning and the quest for meaning.

As part of his general revelation, I believe God is continually making us aware of many of his moral characteristics that should also be characteristics of human beings, created in his image.[56] If a person does not believe in the God of the Bible and rejects God's general revelation, these attributes of God (and humanity) become largely separated in the human mind, so that one person or culture emphasizes love and positive regard of others, while another person or culture emphasizes loyalty to family or clan, while others emphasize justice or honesty. And intellectually serious atheism frequently runs the risk of denying the reality of all these moral values, a tendency which we call nihilism. But once we accept our knowledge of God, we can begin to understand and experience that these attributes and values are unified in the Being of God and in the relationships among the Persons of the Trinity. These attributes should become unified in practice as we are restored in Christ into integrated humanness. And we experience meaning as we both practice and receive these moral values in all our relationships.[57]

---

[56] In the language of academic theology, this topic is sometimes discussed under the heading of "the communicable attributes of God."

[57] In another study of this topic, I have suggested that we Christians experience real meaning before God by means of the transition back and forth between work and worship. See my *Sabbath, Work, and the Quest for Meaning*, MBS Text 162, available online at www.bucer.eu. Click Resources; then click MBS Texts.

Chapter Five: Existential Angst

A serious atheist may say, "This is all so much rubbish! Don't you Christians create an imaginary God so that life does not feel so empty and hopeless?" But I notice that some of the most thoughtful and sensitive descriptions of existential Angst and the loss of meaning have come from the pens of convinced and serious atheists such as Camus and Russell. The loss of meaning is part of the human separation from God, and as part of his general revelation, God continues to ask people, both believers and unbelievers, "Does your life have meaning?" "Is your life totally without purpose?" Some will suppress the question; it simply causes too much Angst. But even when suppressed, this question drives people to try to fill their meaning vacuum with a God-substitute. The writer of Ecclesiastes has tried most of the normal God-substitutes and has found them lacking.

> There is a valuable tradition within Christian philosophy that offers an explanation of meaning that is complementary to what I have offered without being word-for-word identical with what I have written. This view claims that God has created the world in such a manner that creation has many different aspects or dimensions which cannot be reduced to each other, so that in order to understand God's world, we should consider how each aspect or dimension of creation is both distinct from others and also serves other dimensions of creation. Some distinguish 15 or more distinct dimensions of creation, including such different facets as the mathematical, spatial, biological, logical, historical, linguistic, economic, and legal aspects of all of life. For example, when I say, "My wife and I have been married for more than 35 years," I can quickly identify mathematical, biological, logical, historical, linguistic, economic, and legal dimensions of our marriage and of my statement about our marriage. Christian philosophers using this method of analysis often say that meaning is the interconnection of the many different dimensions of God's creation; meaning is the way in which each dimension of creation both serves the other dimensions of God's world and is dependent on the other dimensions of God's world. I agree; this is a valuable part of our response as Christians to the loss of meaning in the modern world.
>
> When people repress their knowledge of God, they frequently treat one dimension of God's creation as if it were truly the most important, as a God-substitute. And when this happens, people do not properly experience the meaningful interconnectedness of the many dimensions of God's creation. For us to fully understand and experience the connected secondary meanings in God's world, we have to understand and experience them in gratitude to God, who provides ultimate meaning. An older but good intro-

> duction to this tradition is L. Kalsbeek, *Contours of a Christian Philosophy: An Introduction to Herman Dooyeweerd's Thought,* Toronto: Wedge, 1975.

Following in the footsteps of Ecclesiastes, previous generations of Christians have sometimes explained the whole Christian message as an answer to the question of meaning. More than 1600 years ago (about 398 A.D.), St. Augustine began his long personal testimony (*The Confessions,* in which he taught much theology and apologetics) with a prayer on the topic of meaning: "Our hearts are restless until they find their rest in You." Much of what Augustine preached and wrote was an answer to the question of the meaning of life. Centuries later the Westminster Shorter Catechism (1647) took a similar step to show the way in which the entire Christian faith is an answer to the question of meaning in life. The first question to be considered is, "What is the chief end of man?", to which the answer is, "Man's chief end is to glorify God and to enjoy Him forever." With this beginning, the writers then explained the central themes of our faith and ethics. We can learn to do something similar today. People are wrestling with the question of meaning because they are wrestling with God's general revelation. The biblical message is the answer to the human quest for meaning.

To rephrase Camus, suicide and the meaning of life are fundamental philosophical questions, but they are primarily questions to be answered by Christian missions (even if the missionary is a philosopher). The biblical message responds to and correlates with existential Angst and the universal quest for meaning. All Christians, who are all missionaries, can learn to address this need, perhaps by simply saying we find our meaning and purpose in relation to God, perhaps by quoting the Catechism. It is valuable in all our relationships and activities to raise the question of meaning and purpose, or even to ask our neighbors, friends, colleagues, and students not only, "What is the meaning of life?" but also, "Why do we ask about the meaning of life?" Without God, we may be left with words like those of Camus and Russell, asking if suicide is rational and thinking that nothing in the universe relates to our hopes, fears, and loves. The biblical message not only explains why we are searching for meaning. It also provides answers we can practice.

Chapter Six: Ontological Angst

On the morning I sat down to write about ontological Angst, I read an article in the news about a scientist, Dmitry Itskov, who plans to develop within only a couple decades a computerized robot into which you can transplant your brain, so that you can go on living when your body is worn out. And only another decade later, he predicts, he will be able to transplant your memory into the robot, without your brain, so "you" can go on living without your body or your brain, so that "you" can live forever.[58] He is promising eternal life for the super wealthy, and I will not be surprised if some people believe his promises. Obviously I placed the word "you" in quotations because I would like to think there is more to "me" than my memories; I regard my body and my brain as part of "me," too.

I then turned to wikiHow and learned "How to Overcome Fear of Death," which offered nine steps contributed by various people.[59] There is now an online "how to" manual for learning how to die properly, meaning how to die without fear! (They, too, have observed that the mortality rate for the human race still seems to be very close to 100%, regardless of medical and technical advances.) These authors were not specifically writing for Christian readers, and it seems that they represented different religions and philosophies of life, yet they included an imprecise quotation of Jesus' words in Matthew 6:34: "Do not worry about tomorrow, for tomorrow will worry for itself. Each day has enough trouble of its own." They perceived the way in which fear of death is not far removed from fear of life. Ontological Angst includes both the fear of death and also the fear of life, meaning worry about our fate in the future; ontological Angst is a deep, sometimes overwhelming concern about what will happen to me (or to us) and whether or not I (or we) will be able to respond appropriately, both in time and in eternity.

We know that our entire being is threatened, ultimately by death (both of ourselves and our loved ones), and that we are threatened secondarily by all that will happen to us and to all that we value. Our fate in this life is always uncertain; realism on this topic is contained in traditional marriage

---

[58] Mike Wehner, "If you live until 2045, you may never have to fear death," *Today in Tech,* August 1, 2012. A caption under a graphic stated, "If you have enough cash, a Russian man may be able to help you live forever." Salvation is now something to purchase, not something to either earn with great moral effort or to receive as a gift from God.

[59] August 3, 2012, http://www.wikihow.com/Overcome-Fear-of-Death

vows in which a man and woman commit to each other "for better or for worse, for richer, for poorer, in sickness and in health," recognizing the uncertainties we all face. It is easy to be afraid of both death and of life, sometimes to the extent that death seems less threatening than life. Obviously this Angst is interconnected with moral Angst, since guilt and shame often enter into our concerns about fate and death; and obviously ontological Angst is interactively related to existential Angst, since fate and death threaten our many particular meanings while existential Angst can lead to contemplating suicide. But ontological Angst must be distinguished from the moral and existential realms of experience as a distinct type of human experience with wide-ranging consequences. Merely the act of writing about the topic sends a shiver through my soul, so that I feel again how uncertain the future is, not only for myself but also for all those I love. Will the future mean illness, pain, poverty, and loneliness?

In the murky depths of human consciousness, regardless of a person's religion or culture, I hear echoes of God's word to Adam in Eden about the tree of the knowledge of good and evil, "when you eat of it, you will surely die." (Genesis 2:17) Death and separation from God are easily and naturally intertwined in the minds of humanity, even for people without the biblical message. After Eden, Adam and Eve died immediately, but they also did not die immediately. Their social/physical life continued, enabled by God's common grace, but their separation from God meant that the God-given goodness of life was always penetrated by the shadow of death, so that alienation, guilt, uncertainty, and meaninglessness influence all of life. This shadow of death penetrating into all of life is ontological Angst.

Jesus addressed this problem when he prayed about his followers, "Now this is eternal life: that they may know you, the only true God, and Jesus Christ, whom you have sent." (John 17:3) Real life means having a positive and accepted knowledge of God in Jesus Christ, knowing I am accepted by God. Merely having my memories continue to function within a computer or robot might be more like hell than eternal life. Would I really want to continue for centuries as a memory within a machine, facing eternal guilt, shame, and meaninglessness, while also fearing that someone might turn off the computer? It is not a sufficient response to ontological Angst, though it illustrates how this type of Angst drives so much of human activity.

The ultimate solutions which people seek for ontological Angst always include an element of naked faith, by which I mean faith that is not extensively based on reason or evidence. When I have stood by the grave of a loved one, both grieving the loss and pondering eternity, my mind has raced through the many reasons I have studied about why people believe the Christian message to be true. In seconds I review the arguments for the existence of God, the evidences for the resurrection of Jesus, and the evidences for the historical truthfulness of the Bible. And every time I have been in that situation, I have come to the same conclusion. The many arguments and evidences are extremely reassuring to know, a real treasure, but Christian arguments and evidences do not reach all the way to the promises which we need when we face ontological Angst. A proof of the existence of God or of the resurrection of Jesus does *not* also prove the promise of Jesus, "My Father's house has many rooms; if that were not so, would I have told you that I am going there to prepare a place for you? And if I go and prepare a place for you, I will come back and take you to be with me that you also may be where I am." (John 14:2-3) My faith feels naked when I believe these words of Jesus as well as the famous words of the apostle Paul when he writes, "For to me, to live is Christ and to die is gain." (Philippians 1:21).

In contrast to such naked faith in God's promises, many of our other Christian convictions are matters of both faith and reason in which faith does not stand naked before God. The proper use of reason leads us to affirm that murder, theft, lying, and adultery are wrong, though these are also matters of faith for all who have read and believed God's Ten Commandments. Thoughtful people often know something about both human dignity and human sinfulness on the basis of reason before they read about these themes in the Bible, though without the biblical narrative they lack a sufficient explanation of what they observe and experience about human nature.[60] A similar joining of faith and reason, so that many of our Christian beliefs are matters of both faith and reason, is true for the many themes addressed by Christian evidences and arguments.

But at the point of our deepest need, ultimate ontological Angst, fear of death, separation, and eternity, we are left with naked faith. We feel the echo of a central theme of God's general revelation echoing through the universe and our entire experience, that "those who do such things are worthy of death." (Romans 1:32) And this drives many of us, much of the human race, to a condition we might call religious panic, panic that might last a moment or might last a lifetime.

Religious panic driven by ultimate ontological Angst not only leads people to believe almost any and every promise, theory, or claim that seems to address this need. (I am thinking here of the way in which people

---

[60] The moral content of what God communicates to us by general revelation can, in principle, be known by moral reason, whereas the gospel is only known by faith.

who may claim to be atheists or materialists, then also believe in spirits, reincarnation, or a personal afterlife reconciled with friends and family.) This type of Angst also lies just below the surface of many of the very worst things that people do, both individually and collectively. Religiously or ideologically motivated violence (and will to power) commonly includes the motive of people trying to gain certainty of eternal life or paradise (or certainty about anything in the future) by means of some extreme or violent act in this life, perhaps by means of suicide or martyrdom. This is ideological extremism or religious fanaticism. Though the general revelation of God's moral law should make it possible for humans to live together in a civilized manner, the Angst produced by our encounter with that generally revealed moral law can also drive us to the worst crimes against humanity.

In my personal experience I find the solution to moments of religious panic by noticing the way in which God has demonstrated his covenant faithfulness for many generations and the way in which both the central events of the gospel and the application of the gospel in our lives are designed to emphasize God's faithfulness to his promises. At least since the time of Abraham, God has unfolded a series of promises which progressively build on what God has done in previous generations. For example, Joseph (Genesis chapters 37-45) could know how God had kept his promises to Abraham, Isaac, and Jacob. Many generations later, King David knew how God kept his promises to his people for many centuries after Abraham, Isaac, Jacob, and Joseph. The birth, death, and resurrection of Jesus, the Messiah, are organic parts of the unfolding and fulfillment of God's covenant faithfulness over many centuries after the time of David. Now the celebration of the Lord's Supper (Holy Communion or Eucharist) in our churches is God's direct confirmation of this covenant *with me* (and, of course, with all believers), to which the Holy Spirit provides internal confirmation by replying inside "Father!" And after worship, in a moment of theoretical reflection, I notice the wonderful way in which God's provision correlates with our deepest Ängste. And I can sing, with the apostle Paul, "Where, O death is your victory? Where, O death, is your sting?" (1 Corinthians 15:55; Paul was referencing Hosea 13:14.)

But we must not forget the importance of secondary ontological Angst, our worry about what will happen to us and to ours in our earthly future. Without this type of Angst, many of our learned people would be without a job. Why is there work for futurologists and horoscope writers, business analysts and tarot card readers, sociologists and psychics, if not for our

Chapter Six: Ontological Angst

worry about life in the future? Of course, our Christian faith addresses this need in the doctrine of the providence of God.

There have been one-sided interpretations of what believers should expect in this life, mistakenly applying promises we should receive in eternity to our earthly future. Promises of total ease and happiness in this life, along with complete health and limitless wealth, attempt to address our Angst in an artificial manner, ignoring one of the promises of Jesus many do not like, "In this world you will have trouble." (John 16:33) A balanced understanding of God's providence is found in an old Protestant text, the Heidelberg Catechism. We are told that God's providence is the way in which he upholds and rules heaven and earth in such a way that "leaves and grass, rain and drought, fruitful and unfruitful years, food and drink, health and sickness, riches and poverty, and everything else, come to us not by chance but by his fatherly hand."[61] Such an approach to our earthly future, filled with confidence that nothing (not even unfruitful years, sickness, or poverty) can separate us from the Father's hand, can give us courage to live and to attempt to find practical solutions to daily problems.

Our neighbors, to whom we are bringing the gospel of Christ, are all wrestling with ontological Angst, which is part of our awareness of our fallen situation. This Angst, as well as the other varieties of Angst, is a human reaction to God's general revelation with its multifaceted content. Many Christians are already comfortable talking about these themes in our prayers, in our Bible studies, and in sermons. We can become comfortable talking about these themes with people who are not yet believers, knowing that the gospel and the entire biblical message is God's response to these deepest human needs. When we talk about Christ, we sometimes have the fear that we are talking about something that is irrelevant and does not interest normal people. Once we understand that everyone around us is struggling with Angst because everyone is wrestling with God's general revelation, we see and feel the relevance and importance of God's special revelation in Christ. Angst is not a psychiatric illness; it is the human condition to which God has responded with the biblical message. This makes the gospel and the rest of the promises of God suddenly seem to be the most important matters in life, equipping us to talk with our neighbors.

---

[61] *Heidelberg Catechism*, answer 27. This classic text was written by two young pastors, Zacharius Ursinus and Caspar Olevianus, published in German in 1563. This quotation is from the 1962 English translation by Allen Miller and Eugene Osterhaven.

Chapter Seven: General Revelation and the Human Quest

Summary: In light of God's general revelation, we can understand the relation between the biblical message and the human quest, the deep drive to understand the universe and our place in it. The human quest arises from the questioning nature of God's general revelation, while God's general revelation both prevents people from completely believing many of the answers that are offered and also contains implied answers so some questions. But the full answer to the human quest is ultimately found in the Bible.

I walk into the fitness center where I am a member in the city of Prague,[62] and I hear the Bloodhound Gang belting out at high decibels over the sound system, "You and me Baby ain't nothin but mammals, so let's do it like they do on the Discovery Channel."[63] At the other end of the room I see new art work on the walls which depicts a sitting Buddha in the midst of scenes that portray the search for a balanced way of life in which the different dimensions of life come into harmony. People are sweating on a treadmill or grunting with heavy weights while they are also wrestling with God in the middle of the human quest; from opposite ends of the room two different answers (the Bloodhound Gang versus the Buddha) are being preached to the questions we all face, one message via music and the other via visual art. And I observe that God is still asking the questions that force people to look for answers, while most do not seem to totally believe the answers they hear coming from the different traditions (hedonistic evolutionism and Buddhism) represented in the room.

Ever since God asked Adam and Eve, "Where are you?" God's general voice in the universe includes questions that seem to unavoidably arise in human experience and cry out for answers. The very fact of human existence forces us to consider the big questions—Who am I? What am I? What

---

[62] The fitness centered described is Svět pod palmovkou, in Prague, Czech Republic. The name translates into English as "The world below a palm tree," an example of Czech humor. Website: http://www.svetpodpalmovkou.cz

[63] In the meantime, things have changed so that one would no longer see frequent mammal mating on the Discovery Channel.

is my place in the world? —while we *also* look for courage in the face of unavoidable Angst. These big questions, which we can call the "Universal Questions," are obviously intertwined with the deepest levels of Angst, yet they are different. These questions are a search for truth, even if the answers found might not sufficiently address our Ängste. Our ability to both appreciate the biblical message and communicate that message to our neighbors will increase if we distinguish the universal questions from Angst. These questions are more cognitive, whereas Angst is more existential, though, of course, our answers to these questions form the building blocks for an entire worldview or philosophy of life which both answers our questions and addresses our Ängste.

Consider this: we are born into the world, or we might say we are thrown into the world,[64] and from our youngest years we find ourselves compelled to try to understand ourselves and our world. We hear answers to our questions offered during our childhood and youth, answers coming from family, neighbors, religions, schools, music, movies, art, and TV. We wonder if we can truly accept the answers offered by our own religion or culture, if we can accept the answers offered by some other religion and culture, or if we must remain confused and uncertain about the universe and ourselves. Because of globalization, like everyone else, we hear answers offered by many different religions and worldviews; each of us has to personally face the big questions that are raised by the experience of existence, and even the decision to hide behind the answers of our own religious or cultural tradition has become a personal decision. This is the human quest in the twenty-first century. Our situation drives us toward spiritual authenticity.

There is always a question/answer relationship between the human quest, our search for answers to life's ultimate questions, and the many particular historical/cultural/religious traditions. Each of the religious, intellectual, and cultural traditions we encounter offers a set of answers to our questions, the Bloodhound Gang versus the Buddha versus many others. This relation between the human quest and history mirrors the relation between Angst and history which was discussed in the previous chapter. This is the question/answer relation between being and history or between existence and history. Life, being, and existence raise questions, and the various historically given religious or secular traditions are always the main source of potential answers to our questions. When we begin to ponder the big questions, most of us listen to the many voices around us, lis-

---

[64] I am borrowing some terms from Martin Heidegger (1889-1976) without endorsing all of his philosophy.

tening for possible answers. And those many potential answers usually come in the form of a narrative or a meta-story which attempts to interpret all of human experience and give direction to all of life. This is why communism, cultural Marxism, Islam, New Age, consumerism, and atheistic evolution are attractive to many. Each offers a big story or a meta-narrative which attempts to answer life's ultimate questions and place one's personal life inside a universal story. And yet, even if people largely accept a story that attempts to answer their quest, they often remain of two minds, deeply uncertain about the narratives they hear. Whether it is the lyrics of Bloodhound Gang or the principles of the Buddha that people "accept," there is always a difference between professed beliefs and practiced beliefs. God's general revelation pushes people to simultaneously presuppose transcendental beliefs about human dignity, the creation order, and the moral law which contradict the lyrics of any other song they sing, so that most cannot fully believe their own words.

Not only does the biblical message, carried by believers, provide real and better answers to the big questions that are raised by existence. The Bible goes much further. It explains why there is this God-given question/answer relation between the human quest and the historically offered answers; it begins to correct the questions; the biblical account explains why the answers to some of our big questions are implicit in God's general revelation which everyone has to use to remain human but which Angst causes people to repress; and, as already emphasized, the Bible explains why people do not fully believe the many inadequate answers.

Remember again that in the opening chapters of the Bible, God's question to Adam and Eve came before the answer. And the answer was the promise of redemption, that the offspring of a woman would crush the head of the serpent. (Genesis 3:15) At first this answer was vague and probably poorly understood, but it showed that the promise of redemption, and really most of the Bible, is the ultimate answer to the problem identified by God's question. God asked a question, "Where are you?" before he offered an answer, showing God's desire for people to be conscious and aware of both their need and the solution which God provides. God is interested in a conscious interaction with us that fully engages our subjectivity. This is part of what God is continuing to do in his general revelation, so that God's pre-missionary work of question-asking comes before our missionary work of giving biblical answers. (Of course, we should recognize that God is the ultimate missionary; we are only secondary missionaries.) And for this reason it is wise for missionaries to both consider how the Bible answers the universal questions and become comfortable discussing these questions at length. In the process of discussing these questions with people who do not yet believe in Christ, their awareness of their status as questioned (by God's general revelation) and their need for answers can be strengthened, while we also offer biblical answers.

For the sake of missionary analysis, as suggested, we will distinguish between Angst-driven questions, such as "Does my life have any meaning?" or "How do I face my guilt and shame?" and quest-driven questions, such as "What is the origin of the world and of human life?" "Why are we all so religious?" "Why do we know more than we want to know about right and wrong?" and "What is a human being?" But we must keep in mind that God's general revelation forms the background for both Angst and for the universal questions. And God's general revelation constantly impinges on the answers to these questions that people consider, because some answers are implied by general revelation, if people dare to consider them. Angst often prevents people from acknowledging truths they know, with a result that people may need to experience the biblical message addressing their Ängste in order to be able to fully acknowledge the truths they know because of general revelation.

In a secular university situation I have used the following list of ten ultimate questions as an illustration of the matters thoughtful people should consider, as illustrations of the human quest. This list is surely neither complete nor perfect, but considering these questions will enable us, as missionaries, to become comfortable discussing these and similar questions.[65]

1. What has always existed? Is it one or is it many? Is it spirit or matter? Is it God or the gods? Is it time and chance? Is it dialectical matter? Is it energy?
2. What does it mean that we are human? What is the morally significant difference between a dog and a human?
3. Why do we know so much about right and wrong? How can it be that people in so many times and places have somewhat similar ideas about right and wrong?
4. How do we know we can usually trust our five senses, even before we have asked if we can trust our senses?

---

[65] I developed this list of questions in response to a university situation that was very consciously secular with elements from communism in the background. University students today seem to be progressively more influenced by various types of mysticism, which may require some further work on questions of this type.

5. How do we know that truth is unified, so that the truths of chemistry do not contradict the truths of biology or mathematics, even before we consider the question?
6. How do we know that other people have minds, even though most of us have never seen a proof of the existence of the minds of other people?
7. Is there something terribly wrong with the world or with human nature? If so, what?
8. Why do we find ourselves alienated from ourselves and each other? Is there a solution?
9. Is being male and female more than an accident of anatomy?
10. Does history have a meaning, direction, or shape? Is it a line, a circle, or something else?

Such universal questions are at the heart of the human quest for truth which we see in literature and philosophy, in religions and ideologies. They occur to thoughtful people who are not too afraid to look for truth. It seems like these questions are asked of us by the universe, but only humans seem to consider these questions. My children raised some of these questions already when they were small; my dog and my computer never discuss these matters with me. Whenever education takes the smallest step beyond basic skills and simple information, which it must do in order to be education suitable for humans, it has to engage such big questions. Even if they are not aware of it, school teachers and university professors are inevitably and significantly influenced by the answers they expect or assume. Just as there is hardly a television show, movie, or popular song in which we do not hear people wrestling with the Angst-laden issues of guilt, forgiveness, meaning, and duty, so also there is hardly a cultural event or educational institution which can avoid considering the big questions that lie in, under, and behind all our Ängste.[66] And because God is the one who asks life's big questions via general revelation as a way of driving people to the answers in special revelation, we see a profound correlation between serious human questions and biblical answers.

---

[66] We are probably all aware that religions and worldviews shape education in schools and universities. In 1986 I became aware of the extent to which worldviews influence museums by visiting the Museum of Modern European History in East Berlin (then under communism). The small displays of artifacts seemed to be overwhelmed by long ideological explanations of the importance of the artifacts in class warfare prior to the time of communism. In the museum I learned a lot about the ideology of East German communism but very little about European history.

During my career teaching religions, ethics, and philosophy in secular universities, largely with students who have not been Christians, I have chosen to emphasize questions of this type, hopefully with flexibility and creativity, as they arise in the many different fields of university study. Such questions have come naturally into the classroom discussion whether the theme of the course has been philosophy of religion, political theory, medical ethics, the history of ethics, or the history of Christianity. I have chosen to emphasize questions of this sort because I believe God is asking such questions through his general revelation, with which most people have a very complicated relationship; discussing such questions has been my attempt to follow God's example in the Garden of Eden (and to build on what I believe God is already doing) by leading with questions before talking about answers. I have tried to use a Socratic method of classroom teaching similar to what I believe the apostle Paul utilized in Romans 2:1-5.

While discussing these questions in a university classroom, I remember that students (like all people) are not only asked these questions by God's general revelation; they already know the answers to many of the questions because of the rich content of general revelation, but they hold that knowledge in a rejected or repressed status in their minds and hearts. For this reason I have chosen to move very slowly from life questions to biblical answers, allowing wrestling time, so students can quietly consider why they know some of the answers but do not want to recognize that they know the answers.[67] These questions merit further consideration in this light.

1. **What has always existed? Is it one or is it many? Is it spirit or matter? Is it God or the gods? Is it time and chance? Is it dialectical matter? Is it energy?** When I have asked students, "What has

---

[67] Much of my university teaching has been in the countries that were once under communism. Some of the popular resentment toward communists arose because many people felt like the communists always told people what to think and what to do, consistently based on the communist ideology, robbing people of the opportunity to think for themselves, thereby treating people as less than fully human. Students have reported to me in strong language that university professors, regardless of their philosophy of life, tend to tell students what to think, not how to think, thereby also treating students as less than fully human. This stands in stark contrast with the method of education that God uses, as described in Genesis and Romans. I have found it very satisfying when students have reported that I have taught them how to think, not what to think, while also communicating the Christian faith in a manner that shows its relevance for the widest range of questions.

Chapter Seven: General Revelation and the Human Quest 85

always existed?" I then go on to mention some of the possible answers that normally occur to people in different cultures, emphasizing that whatever answer one believes, that answer has to truly explain the world and our experience of the world. Depending on the pattern of classroom discussion, I have pointed out that it is difficult to imagine that our experience of knowledge, hope, love, personality, and concern for justice is fully explained either by an impersonal source of the universe (such as matter, energy, and chance) or by polytheism (which lacks an explanation for the unity of the universe and the unity of knowledge). Sometimes I say that the claim that matter, energy, and chance are the three entities that have always existed is very similar to polytheism, because this view posits multiple eternal entities. During the discussion, I assume that all people know, but may pretend not to know, about God's eternal power and divine nature, so that this discussion should prompt serious spiritual discomfort. Of course, my Christian answer to the question is centered in the doctrine of the Trinity, that the unity of God as the source of all that exists explains the unified nature of the universe and truth, while the eternal relationships among the Father, Son, and Holy Spirit explain the way in which relationships (and relational values like love, justice, and honesty) have an ultimate source and place of existence. On occasion in a university classroom, I have pointed out that the doctrine of the Trinity is the solution to the question about the relation between the "One" and the "Many," which shows that both unity and multiplicity have equal ultimacy.[68] But in a university classroom I sometimes choose not to answer the question, "What has always existed?" because I want the students to wrestle further with the truths which they know but cannot admit to knowing. According to the apostle Paul, my students already know the answer to the question. I have also discovered that some university students become curious about me personally and Google me, with a result that they have a printed version of a Christian article I had written in their backpacks while they are discussing philosophy

---

[68] Solutions to the question of the "One" and the "Many" which say the "One" is truly ultimate tend to correspond with totalitarian or collectivist social/political theories, whereas solutions that say the "Many" are truly ultimate tend to correspond with individualistic social/political theories. A Trinitarian solution corresponds with saying both the collective and the individual are real but emphasizes our relations with each other in multiple social organizations and institutions.

with me in a secular university classroom. After class they have felt free to talk more openly about their questions.

2. **What does it mean that we are human? What is the morally significant difference between a dog and a human?** When I have asked students what it means to be human and how are they different from my dog (My wife and I have had a series of boxers for many years.), only very rarely has any student said that there is no morally significant difference between humans and animals. As a result of being created in God's image, and as a part of God's ongoing general revelation, people have a direct intuition and knowledge that humans are distinct in the universe and carry a special type of dignity which deserves respect. This God-given direct intuition stands in tension with what many people in secular universities are taught to believe about human nature (which is often related to atheistic versions of evolutionary theory), while at the same time, this God-given intuition stands behind the concerns for human rights which are affirmed by so many people. If people affirm human dignity, then one cannot avoid the question of the source of that dignity; if people deny human dignity, then why should we not devour each other like animals? When lecturing on human nature and human rights, I have sometimes chosen to make the prayer from Psalm 8:3-8 one of my first references to the Bible as the answer to the human quest: "When I consider your heavens, the work of your fingers, the moon and the stars, which you have set in place, what is mankind that you are mindful of them, human beings that you care for them? You have made them a little lower than the angels and crowned them with glory and honor. You made them rulers over the works of your hands; you put everything under their feet: all flocks and herds, and the animals of the wild, the birds in the sky, and the fish in the sea, all that swim the paths of the seas." These words provide a beautiful answer to the longing to understand oneself which many people feel but cannot explain without the biblical message. I strongly affirm the common Christian observation that knowing God leads to truly knowing ourselves (and other humans) and that truly knowing ourselves truly can also lead to knowing God. Sometimes the first step toward accepting the Christian faith is for a person to begin to put into words his previously unformulated intuitions that humans are distinct in the universe and that the Bible gives an explanation of this distinctiveness.

3. **Why do we know so much about right and wrong? How can it be that people in so many times and places have had somewhat similar ideas about right and wrong?** When I raise the question of why we know so much about right and wrong I sometimes phrase the question, "Why do we know more about right and wrong than we want to know?" In light of what we learn from Romans 1, we know that people are not ignorant about right and wrong; the problem in ethics is that people do not like what they know about right and wrong because of God's general revelation, and therefore people cannot fully explain what they know about right and wrong without explicitly mentioning God. And once we mention God as the source of our moral knowledge, all the reactions related to moral Angst become more prominent. The most common responses about the source of moral knowledge I have heard in university classrooms have been some variety of culturally based moral relativism which claims moral rules only arise from a particular culture and do not have global validity. Of course, there are some morally important matters that are culturally relative, meaning that it is morally required of us to learn the local rules and to follow them. (A good example is whether one has to drive on the right or the left hand side of the road; there is no absolute and universal rule about which side of the road to drive, but it is obviously immoral not to know and follow the local rules since one might kill someone if he does not follow the culturally relative rules.) One must recognize this area of moral relativity, even though it is often strongly overemphasized, to have an honest conversation. But in the secular universities where I have taught, students tend to say everything is morally relative, meaning that right and wrong depend entirely on local expectations, and then, without recognizing the self-contradiction, they go on to assume that everyone knows he must not break a short list of rules, such as not murdering, not stealing, not raping, not committing cannibalism, and perhaps not deceiving other people. (Only once did I meet a student who seriously claimed it is morally acceptable for a culture to practice cannibalism. I have heard much more uncertainty about whether or not truth telling is morally required.) Then one can ask, "Why do people say everything is morally relative, even though they do not really think everything is morally relative?" and "What does this internal contradiction tell us about human nature and about the universe?" At this point in the discussion, I think it is sometimes best to let people wrestle with the questions,

not giving answers too quickly, because I believe such people are wrestling directly with God.

4. **How do we know we can usually trust our five senses, even before we have asked if we can trust our senses?** Most of the students I have taught have had little doubt that they can trust their five senses under normal circumstances, but only rarely have students had any explanation of why they think their senses give them truth about the universe or how it is that the human race has come to trust its five senses. (If I remember correctly, every answer to this question I have heard from students in a philosophy classroom has involved students telling a story about the origins and development of the human race as a part of evolution.) Though the topic merits further explanation, I believe, very briefly stated, that we can trust our senses because God created us so that there is a three-way natural correlation among our senses, the categories of understanding in our minds, and the universe outside our minds; and God gives us direct awareness of this correlation as part of his general revelation, so much that many people never even consider why they trust their senses. Once the question becomes explicit, it pushes people to begin to recognize the role that God plays in our lives, even if we try to deny or ignore him. God's continuing general revelation is the ultimate condition (behind several secondary conditions) that enables our normal human experience of knowing we can usually trust our senses. I have known a few students who were inclined to say they were skeptics in regard to their five senses, an inclination which leads a few people into deep personal problems. Therefore, I have not usually asked students, "Can you trust your five senses?" Instead I usually phrase the question in terms something like, "Why is it that you know you can trust your senses?" This phrasing tends to point people toward the hidden theological assumptions in their daily process of knowing the world around them.

5. **How do we know that truth is unified, so that the truths of chemistry do not contradict the truths of biology or mathematics, even before we consider the question?** In the developed world, everyone seems to assume there are real truths in realms such as chemistry, biology, physics, and mathematics; further, everyone seems to assume that the truths in these areas are unified, meaning that the truths in chemistry do not contradict the truths in biology, nor the truths of physics, nor the truths of mathematics. This assumption about the unity of truth makes technological development

possible. While everyone makes these normal academic assumptions, at the very same time, some people deny we can know true truth about the universe. And on serious reflection, almost everyone has to admit that normal people do not learn about this unity of truth in the natural sciences by means of scientific experimentation or other uses of their five senses. The unity of truth in natural science is an expectation that we bring to the process of science. There is much about the existence, nature, and unity of truth that people very commonly assume (even if a few claim to deny these truths), and I believe this is right to do because these truths are part of God's general revelation which makes normal human experience possible. At first, some people have difficulty grasping these questions because they seem very theoretical, and some people resist asking such questions because they secretly want to suppress their knowledge of God. But these questions arise to thoughtful people because God is questioning us in a manner that drives us to recognize his role in human life. Many Christians can learn to discuss these questions in a manner that makes the questions more explicit and helps people to consider the biblical answers.

6. **How do we know that other people have minds, even though most of us have never seen a proof of the existence of the minds of other people?** I have used the question about proving the existence of the minds of other people for a specific purpose within western universities: to illustrate the need to reform some models of what knowledge is, which dominate our educational systems, that have been inappropriately used in relation to God. Since the time of the Enlightenment (starting around 1650), educational systems following the western model have used models of proving knowledge that are very good in relation to knowing physical things, whether building a bridge that is safe or curing medical problems. Whether in a school or a scientific laboratory, we commonly think we know something either on the basis of empirical evidence or on the basis of logical/mathematical proof. The relevant question inside this perspective is whether we are using inductive or deductive reasoning. This approach to knowing is very beneficial for everyday knowledge, reducing the amount of dangerous nonsense that people believe, thereby contributing massively to scientific and technological development. However, this method of knowing has been inappropriately applied to knowing about the non-physical realm. Thereby it easily becomes an important way in which people supp-

ress their direct knowledge of God, making it easier for people to say that they do not know God even though they really do know God. (In a philosophy class, I describe this problem as classical or narrow foundationalism.) One step toward showing that this valuable model of knowledge is commonly used in an inappropriate manner is to show that we do not, cannot, and should not use this model of knowing in relation to other people. There may not be any totally satisfactory inductive or deductive proof that the important people in our lives in fact have minds, but we all know that our loved ones (and even people we do not like) really have minds much like our own. And if someone invents a real proof for the existence of the minds of other people, that proof may be too complex for us ordinary people to understand. The problem here is in the model of what we describe as real knowledge within our educational systems, not with any real uncertainty that my wife, children, or grandchildren have minds. It is our certainty about the reality of the minds of other people that makes it possible to reevaluate the way we claim to gain certainty of knowledge in education and scientific research. Every day everyone uses methods of knowing other people that do not fit into our Enlightenment models of knowledge, and we all think this is perfectly proper because it is necessary for our daily lives, because we assume that the method of knowing has to correspond to the area of knowledge. So, too, I have argued in university classes, we should not use Enlightenment models of scientific knowing in order to claim we cannot know God. While discussing this philosophical argument that sounds technical, I assume my students are really wrestling with God, so that my role is to simply take away one of the educational tools some have been using to defend against God's direct claim on their lives.[69]

7. **Is there something terribly wrong with the world or with human nature? If so, what?** When discussing this question in secular university classrooms, it is my impression from student reactions that many have considered the question, though the question itself is in tension with much of secular thought. It is commonly said today that we cannot learn or derive "ought" from "is," or, conversely, that we cannot learn "ought not" from "is." This is one of the principles of modern and postmodern culture that everyone is supposed

---

[69] For a good introduction to the problems of narrow foundationalism, see Ronald H. Nash, *Faith & Reason: Searching for a Rational Faith* (Grand Rapids: Zondervan, 1988), pp. 69-92.

to know and follow which is consistent with believing in atheistic evolution and with any worldview that does not see any purpose in the universe. But very few people (if any) honestly follow this principle. Most people think there is something terribly wrong with the world or with human nature or that something must be done to make the world a better place. We all see or read reports of suffering, oppression, and the inhumanity of man against man and immediately feel that something is wrong or that something must be changed. Everyone seems to know that what is ought not to be, thereby denying a cardinal principle of secular education in the western world that few people really believe. (This reminds me of the situation in the communist countries of Eastern Europe during the last decades of communism. Everyone was supposed to believe the communist ideology, but many people knew that few people honestly believed the required ideology.) And once we begin to discuss this question sensitively, people are again driven to quietly ponder why they ask this question and how they know important truths that are inconsistent with unbelief. God is continuously and quietly asking, "Adam and Eve, what is wrong with you?" By openly raising the question in an educational situation, we push people to consider the question more vigorously. And the people with whom we are working will probably soon discover what we believe is the answer.

8. **Why do we find ourselves alienated from ourselves and each other? Is there a solution?** I find it amazing that so many people are able to describe alienation so brilliantly. Students often describe truly horrible conflicts between their mother and their father, and then they describe a deep separation of themselves from their parents. I have sat and listened to reports in which the student talking with me thought a murder in the family was a real and present danger. What is amazing is that, in the process, almost everyone communicates an overwhelming sense that this is not the way things should be, often mixed with hope for improvements or even for reconciliation, even though his sense that there is a such a thing as healthy relationships and his hope for reconciliation contradicts his entire worldview. What is important for our mission philosophical purposes is to notice that everyone assumes, usually without any qualifications, that conflict and alienation are bad and present a problem to be solved, not that conflict and alienation simply are. If, as the Bloodhound Gang claims, we are nothing but mammals, the most we could very seriously claim is that one does not *like* conflict

and alienation, while our social scientists investigate whether alienation helps or hurts the economy.[70] But almost no one ever says that conflict and alienation simply are. Everyone I have ever heard describe conflict and alienation assumes we all know something significant about what peaceful, wholesome relationships look like, even if he has not seen peaceful relationships and his basic worldview would say that conflict simply is, not that conflict is bad. I believe there is still an echo in the human heart of the time in the Garden of Eden (before Adam and Eve were alienated from God, from themselves, from each other, and from the rest of creation), which gives significant hints about what non-alienated relationships with each other, with God, and with the environment should look like. Part of being human is to not only know what alienation and conflict are but also to sense, perhaps vaguely, that conflict and alienation should not exist. By phrasing the question "Why do we find ourselves alienated from ourselves and each other?" we can easily move to the question of why we are able to recognize alienation as alienation and to know that alienation and conflict should not exist. Phrasing the question in this manner also allows us to very easily enter into dialogue with the descriptions of alienation coming from many philosophers, sociologists, and journalists. Some of my students in Eastern Europe know the penetrating sociological descriptions of alienation that Karl Marx penned as a young man, descriptions which moved Marx to look for something better for society as a whole, really a type of redemption, though few of my students have believed that the revolution of the proletariat that Marx prophesied would provide that redemption.[71] Talking about alienation is a way to remind people of something they know but may have pushed from their minds. In looking at Romans 1:27, we notice that a theme in God's general revelation is the creation order or scheme of life that refers back to the mandates given in creation

---

[70] I am convinced that family conflict and the breakup of marriages contribute to many other social problems, including economic problems at the level of entire national economies, but that is a theme for another study.

[71] I am thinking here of Karl Marx's *Economic and Philosophical Manuscripts* of 1844 in which he described four types of alienation: the alienation of a worker from the product of his labor, from the act of producing, from himself as a worker, and from his fellow workers. Many have observed that Marx was both influenced by and alienated from the Jewish and Christian religions. I believe his theory of alienation was possible because of an echo of the Garden of Eden in the human heart which is maintained by God's continuing general revelation.

and thereby to the conditions in the Garden of Eden before the fall of the human race. Talking about alienation is a step toward people seeing themselves as questioned by God, "Adam and Eve, why are you separated from everything?" This can lead to seeing their need for redemption in Christ, not only reconciliation in relation to each other and in relation to the rest of creation.

9. **Is being male and female more than an accident of anatomy?** The university students I have taught in the post-communist world have generally come from a background which has included a partial definition of gender roles and identity but that has been marked by a huge amount of family dysfunction and frequent divorce. At the same time, the educational system is increasingly marked by an understanding of humanness with a very problematic understanding of the relation between a person's body and a person's self. Whereas at one time many held the opinion that one is his body, assuming our bodies are the entirety of our humanness, more now seem to think that one's real self (usually meaning what was called the soul or the spirit in previous generations) exists in total independence from the body. Within this recent way of thinking, a female self might accidentally be born with a male body, or a male self might accidentally be born with a female body. Though I find this way of thinking very strange, it fits with (and may result from) ways of understanding human nature in our cultural and religious history that describe the distinction of the soul from the body as too large. I believe God created me as a male soul and a male body, though I do not understand how God weaves a body and soul together to make the complete whole we call a person. But some of the alienation from the self that people experience exists at this level; it is part of our alienation from the entirety of God's creation order. I believe people are questioned by God's general revelation in this realm. Obviously one has to be very careful while discussing this theme, since it can be far more personal than a question such as "How do we know that truth is unified?" For some people, questions about gender identity are closely tied with both moral and existential Angst; guilt, shame, and a loss of personal meaning can overshadow both the question and possible answers. Some people appear to look for meaning by means of saying something about themselves that may be intended to shock others. Because of the subjects I have taught at the university level, this question has arisen less frequently in the classroom than have some other universal questions. How-

ever, it is one of the questions for which people need biblical answers combined with a reconciling relationship with other people and with God.
10. **Does history have a meaning, direction, or shape? Is it a line, a circle, or something else?** Existential Angst, the sense that life might not have any meaning, leads people to wonder if the history of the human race or the history of the universe is coming from somewhere or going somewhere. In some form or another, every worldview, religion, and ideology presents a big story which tries to shed light and meaning on one's personal, small story. Many from the past and the present think the world goes through a circular process that is repeated many times, perhaps an infinite number of times, in a process of millions or billions of years. The communists claimed that history moves from feudalism through capitalism into socialism by means of the class struggle, giving meaning to the life of the individual according to the person's place in the inevitable flow of history. Jews and Christians, influenced by the Bible, think of history as a finite line from creation to final judgment; of course, we should say that the fall accomplished by Adam and Eve and the redemption accomplished by Christ are also decisive steps in the process of history. In my years teaching in secular universities, I found that most students have been very comfortable talking about views of history (without high levels of Angst), and most understood that it is a fundamental question that everyone should answer. Curiously, most of the North American and European students I have taught have openly acknowledged that their views of history are linear and shaped by the Bible, even if they were atheists. Most have simply accepted a linear view of history as being as much a part of the western cultural inheritance as democracy is and have recognized the communist view of history as a heresy based on the western view. Yet the biblical answer, which sees God as the Creator and Sustainer of history and Judge at the end of history, is an answer which produces overwhelming Angst if one does not know the biblical gospel of salvation in Christ. The real answer to the direction and shape of history is the biblical account of creation, fall, redemption, and final return of Christ; the question occurs for many thoughtful people.

The human quest is closely associated with Angst, our awareness of our fallenness. We find ourselves threatened by life in the world (ontologically, morally, and existentially), while we are also questioned by the universe.

Chapter Seven: General Revelation and the Human Quest

While there will be many secondary causes in the life of each person and culture, it is important that we understand that God's general revelation is the ultimate cause behind this entire consciously threatened and questioned nature of human life. Even if some aspects of my interpretation of Angst and being questioned need significant improvement, we can see an overview of one important relationship of the biblical message to human experience: the Bible stands in an answering relationship to fallen life, with all its Ängste and questions. Knowing this should help equip us for bringing the biblical message to our neighbors who need it.

Chapter Eight: Selected Questions in the Philosophy of Religion in Light of God's General Revelation

There are several themes that become clear and questions that are answered when we emphasize the way in which people are wrestling with God's general revelation. Some of these questions have been perceived to be problems for Christians, especially when we take up the missions calling God has given us. Considering these questions will enrich our understanding of God's general revelation and its role in the lives of all people.

A. Religions as Replacements

In light of God's general revelation and the human response, we can understand why many religions and worldviews have themes that are replacements for themes in the Bible.

The scene in classical Greek mythology in which Agamemnon sacrifices his own daughter, Iphigenia, to the goddess Artemis in order to gain the favor of the deity is so heart-rending that most people today step back in horror at the entire notion of human sacrifice. But the story illustrates the way in which many people are aware of a need for a sacrifice to have peace with the divine. As Christians we believe that the one true sacrifice, to which all other sacrifices point, was the self-sacrifice of the God-Man, Jesus. There has only ever been one legitimate human sacrifice in all of human history, when Jesus offered himself to die on the cross at the hands of sinful humanity. Under the influence of the cross, human sacrifice has become much less common around the entire world. But the way in which other religions include sacrificial rituals illustrates the way in which many religions have themes that replace biblical themes.

Something similar can be said about the need for moral or religious purification. Many religions have a ritual for purification; bathing in the Ganges River in India may be the most well-known. Our Muslim neighbors also have rituals for purification which one should practice in order to pray properly. And the Old Testament law included numerous rules and rituals regarding purification; the whole system of various sacrifices can be seen as a system of national and personal purification. In a broad but imprecise pattern, because of the questions and anxieties arising from the human encounter with God's general revelation, people create beliefs and practices that tend to replace biblically inspired beliefs and practices. Opponents of the Christian faith have sometimes said that the similarity in themes between the Christian faith and other religions means that the Christian faith is not unique and therefore not true. But this attack on Christian belief is reversed, if people cannot avoid wrestling with the God of the Bible. The biblical message is the only message which properly addresses our deepest questions and Ängste, but because any religion or philosophy of life has to address those same needs, the many religions tend to have themes that mimic biblical themes. A humorously extreme example was the communist ritual of welcoming baby citizens, an obvious replacement for Christian rituals welcoming babies into the church which the communist political parties in some countries were consciously trying to replace.

This replacement character of idolatry was already addressed in the Old Testament. In Psalm 130:7 we read, "O Israel, put your hope in the Lord, for with the Lord is unfailing love and with him is full redemption." The unstated assumption of this and similar texts is that if the people do not find their hope in God, they will find their hope somewhere else. People always put their hope in something or someone, and if people do not put their hope in God, they will put their hope in someone or something that God has created. Idolatry involves replacement.

It is interesting to notice that when the people of Israel made the golden calf, the typical illustration of idolatry in the Old Testament (Exodus 32), they called the idol "the Lord," and they said the idol had brought them out of Egypt. But their purpose in saying this was not primarily to say something about the past. They were anxious about the future (ontological Angst). They were expressing their trust that the calf would save them again in the future. The short summary of the religion of the golden calf would be "The calf saves!" The calf was a replacement for God as the one who would lead them into the future.

To address the experience of Angst and being questioned by life, people put their faith and hope in all sorts of "creators" and "saviors." People are looking for comfort, joy, and meaning, and some will turn to a traditional religion while others turn to wealth, security, adventure, freedom, or sex. And the stories we hear in advertising, popular culture, education, and politics tend to be a series of false gospels, with one person after the next proclaiming how a particular idol will provide hope and fill the empty spot in the hearts of our neighbors and friends. Of course, as previously emphasized, people tend not to fully believe all these false gospels, for in a distorted way they know something of the truth of God. And it is this distorted, repressed general revelation of God that keeps them searching for something to fill the gospel-shaped vacuum in the human heart and mind.

Repressed general revelation, with the resulting anxieties and questions, makes people irrepressibly religious. Creating religions is a human necessity, and among the many religions and worldviews, one quickly detects a compulsion to give an account of both creation and redemption. At the core of alternate religions there is normally a pseudo-redemptive promise that speaks to the inner religious needs of men and women, a substitute gospel, as well as an alternate hypothesis about the origins of the world, a substitute for a Creator, perhaps even raising Time, Energy, Matter, and Chance to the status of divinity. Our misbelieving minds continually create new redeemers and new creators to answer our questions and address our ultimate anxieties.

In consumerism it is not difficult to observe a strong tendency to make wealth or prosperity a redeemer substitute. When Jesus talked about the "deceitfulness of wealth" (Matthew 13:22), he was probably thinking that wealth makes a deceitful or deceptive promise to make us happy or secure. This indicates that redeemer substitutes may contain a deceptive or deceitful promise, causing us to think we hear a promise from some part of creation when, in fact, only God himself can make such a promise. When people suppress the knowledge of God given in general revelation, they cannot cease to be religious; faith turns to replacements.

It is painful for some to acknowledge, but the need to have a highest authority is an organic part of our religious nature as humans. Sometimes Christians have been mocked because they recognize the Bible as their highest authority, but such mocking betrays a serious lack of self-awareness. One of the unavoidable questions we face, which intellectually mature people cannot ignore, is that of our highest authority for what we claim to know. If God and his revelations are not acknowledged as our authority, something else becomes an authority, frequently some particular human being (whether Marx, Mao, or Mohammed) or some dimension of our common humanity (perhaps reason or feeling).[72] The important question is not if it is reasonable to believe in an authority; I am convinced that everyone believes in an authority, even if some people cannot identify their highest authority. Belief in an authority is an inescapable human necessity. The important question is which supposed authority is worthy of our ultimate trust.

---

[72] This type of claim has been common in Christian thought at least since the time of Augustine. See Ronald H. Nash, *The Light of the Mind: St. Augustine's Theory of Knowledge* (Academic Renewal Press, 2003), pp. 26, 27.

B. General Revelation and "Proving God"

Sometimes Christians think they have to prove the existence of God and then say that the revelation of God in nature makes it possible for us to develop such proofs. This is the main source of the long tradition of arguments for the existence of God. According to this way of thinking, our natural knowledge of God (which comes separate from the gospel) is largely indirect and is received by means of rational reflection on creation. One commonly hears presentations which argue that the existence of design in the universe indicates the existence of a Designer, along with an extensive series of similar arguments. On the other hand, other believers have thought that the revelation of God in creation is largely inside ourselves, within the human mind and heart. According to this second way of thinking, our natural knowledge of God (which comes separate from the gospel) is direct and intuitive, analogous to our relationships with other people, perhaps without much reflection and without arguments for the existence of God. Why would we waste the effort to develop philosophical proofs for the existence of God any more than we do for family members, since the way we know them is so similar?

In light of Romans 1, I believe there is a direct self-revelation of God that is taken into human consciousness and which provides a necessary condition for all of human experience. This is much closer to what I described in the previous paragraph as the "second way." However, it would not be wise for us to exclusively follow either of these parts of the Christian tradition, without any regard for the other part of the tradition. Paul's way of thinking includes *both* a revelation in nature outside humanity that provides a basis for rational reflection about God and also a general revelation of God within human nature, meaning inside the human mind and heart created in the image of God, which leads to a direct or intuitive knowledge of God. God is revealing himself both through nature and through human nature created in his image, both directly and indirectly, with the result that our knowledge of God coming through creation is multifaceted and received into consciousness in multiple ways, at different levels of our cognitive structure. One of these ways is a direct awareness or sense of his divine nature.[73] Such a direct awareness of God does not mean that proofs for the existence of God are totally irrelevant, just as it is not irrelevant to ask if we need proofs for the existence of people we meet. But if God is actively revealing himself to all people, with the result that

---

[73] This was traditionally called the *sensus divinitatis* in Latin.

knowledge of God is taken into consciousness by all people, this should influence how we consider and use arguments for the existence of God.[74]

Every argument for the existence of God used by a gospel-believing Christian is very deeply *ad hominem*,[75] but not in the customary sense in which we say an *ad hominem* argument is not logically valid because it merely attacks a person making a truth claim without considering the truth claim independently from the merits of the person making the truth claim. In a far deeper sense, if an argument for the existence of God is addressed to a person who claims to be an atheist, and if that "atheist" already knows he or she deserves condemnation for breaking God's moral law, that argument for the existence of God is a profound attack on that person's sense of well-being and entire philosophy of life. In this distinctive and special sense, all arguments for the existence of the God of the Bible are properly *ad hominem;* arguments for the existence of God, especially in the cultural context of western secularism, are really attacks on a person's entire life and set of spiritual defense mechanisms by which that person tries to address Angst and all the ultimate questions. We should use arguments for the existence of God, not because God needs proof, but because an increase in cognitive dissonance can be a contributing factor in a person coming to the accepted knowledge of God by faith in Christ.

A risk involved in rational proofs for the existence of God arises from the human tendency to expect God to be a lot like something in creation. If we have deep habits of worshipping something in creation in place of God, our "proofs" of God may accidentally make it sound like God is not very different from his creation, neglecting God's holiness. Proofs of God, similar to those used by Christians, have also been used by both pantheists (the ancient Stoics) and by deists (especially during the eighteenth century); these "gods" tend to either be not truly infinite (in the case of deism) or not truly distinct from creation (in the case of pantheism). If God is declaring himself through creation, and if the main "proofs" describe God as much less than he is, those proofs can become part of our defensive attempt to hide from God. The gods proved by the normal philosophical proofs are both much less comforting and less frightening than the God of Moses, Isaiah, and Paul.

---

[74] In some university classrooms, I have sometimes said that I believe in reason because I think God exists, rather than claiming I believe in God on the basis of reason. I have said this partly to provoke discussion among students who might think that belief in God has to be the result of reason, but it is what I believe.

[75] In classes on fallacies of reasoning, this is a commonly described mistake which attacks a person to avoid considering the arguments presented by that person.

A closely related problem is the way most arguments for the existence of God depend on different methods of proving something to be true or false, and then these methods continue to play an authoritative role in the hearts and minds of people. My "proof" by which I prove whether or not God may exist then becomes a control belief or cognitive filter which lets me know what else I may or may not believe in many areas of faith and life.[76] This method of proving God can easily influence how we interpret the Bible. And this method of proving God can then shape how we think about the entire relationship between faith and learning, really, the relationship between God and life. We have to be careful when we attempt to prove God; our method of proof can become an authority that replaces the authority of God.

Nevertheless, it is not wise for Christians to stop considering the proofs for God, for they have multiple valuable functions in our faith and life. They help exalt our minds to perceive certain aspects of his Being; they assist us in the important process of developing our knowledge of God at all levels of our cognitive structure (as the Alpha and the Omega of existence); and the arguments for the existence of God continue to provoke cognitive dissonance (wrestling!) for many atheists. These are some of the reasons I have taught philosophy classes on the proofs for the existence of God in secular universities. I think the proofs may be used by the Holy Spirit to bring some to the Father's house while they can also have a constructive influence in the lives of Christians.

However, let the missionary be very careful of the dangers to our souls that arise from our apologies for God. As soon as we "prove God," we silently make ourselves or our hearers the judges of whether or not God has the right to exist, making ourselves gods in place of God, the very worst form of idolatry. Forget not that God is our Judge, even when we play his lawyer and advocate. And when we succeed and prove God, what kind of God have we demonstrated? Is not the God whom many have proved to exist much like any other object of ordinary knowledge in the realm of creation, safe and harmless, surely not a God of wrath? Do not many proofs of God and his revelation tend to eliminate the massive gulf between the Creator and the creation, so that we imagine that we are peering at God through our microscopes or our telescopes, not realizing that we are the ones being observed? Knowing God properly requires of us a profound change in the subject/object relation; knowing God means recognizing that

---

[76] In the academic literature of philosophy this problem is sometimes described as an example of "classical foundationalism" and in academic theology as "Cartesian theology."

we are the "objects" (without denying our subjectivity) who are known by God, who is the real Subject.

And let the missionary beware of our cultural captivity. Whenever we set out to prove God, we do so according to the canons, expectations, and assumptions of a particular culture. The particular culture from which I originate has its rules about what I may or may not believe. These are my control beliefs and cognitive filters, those things I regard as rational or indubitable because of when and where I grew up. When I prove God on the basis of the control beliefs of my culture, even if I call it "pure reason," I have proved a God who is acceptable to my culture; and my control beliefs become a hidden authority which determines what God may be, what he may say, and what he may do. Is it surprising that our "Christianity" has become captive to the culture of modernity and postmodernity? Surely real repentance and conversion will require repentance from the idolatrous control beliefs of our cultures, including those we have used to prove God. Then what will provide the rational foundation on top of which we may prove whether or not God is allowed to exist?

We can be grateful that God is speaking through his creation so our proofs of God are not really proofs. The solution is to rearrange the furniture in the courtroom in our minds. It is not God who is on trial. It is we who are on trial, where we stand naked, without an apology. We need a gospel.

C. General Revelation and Reason

Paul's claim that all people know significant content about God and his moral law from general revelation is crystal clear. Consistent with this conviction, we should infer that many other things that all people know also come from general revelation. Different philosophers may call these truths *common sense ideas*, or *the first principles of reason* (both practical and theoretical reason), or *the transcendental conditions of human experience*. They are the truths that we need to know to carry on our everyday lives but which we cannot learn from our five senses. (The truths we learn from our five senses also have their origin in God, but we receive those truths in a different manner.) It is possible for some people and some cultures to deny that we know these truths (perhaps calling their worldview relativism, nihilism, skepticism, or extreme multiculturalism), but then, as repeatedly mentioned, there is an unavoidable human tendency to act as if we know many truths learned from God's general revelation.

How is it that all people seem to know that we can usually trust our five senses to tell us truth about the everyday world; that two plus two will still equal four tomorrow; that people generally know what love, honesty, justice, and loyalty are and that all people should follow such moral principles? How do we know that the world still exists when we are sleeping, or how do we know that other people have minds something like our own? Why do so many of us have the intuition that humans have a distinct dignity and place in the universe, prior to receiving an explanation of that dignity and role in the universe from a religion or an ideology? How is it that people know that simple logical deductions generally correspond to the real world? How do people know that the truths of chemistry will not contradict the truths of mathematics or biology (the unity of truth)? Why is it that some readers will think these deep questions are almost too stupid to consider? Because all people have a significant body of knowledge that makes everyday human (not merely animal) life possible, knowledge that comes to us from God's general revelation. These are the truths that people should call "reasonable," but reasonable in the sense that they make the use of reason possible, not in the sense that they we learn these truths by means of pure reason.

Short Definitions/Illustrations:
1. "Common Sense Ideas" in this context means things like believing that the world we perceive is real, that our senses and mind correspond to that world, and therefore we can have true knowledge about the world.
2. The "First Principles of Practical Reason" are primary ethical distinctions and duties such as "do good and avoid evil."
3. My preferred term is "the transcendental conditions of human experience," by which I am referring to the several areas and contents which people know only by means of God's direct general revelation.

This means that ordinary people, regardless of their religion, all those who are not psychopaths or insane, in fact trust their reason and senses because of truths received from general revelation. And those truths are organic parts of their unacknowledged knowledge of God. When I say, "I trust my reason and senses because God tells me to trust them" (not that I believe in God on the basis of reason), I am only acknowledging an unavoidable depth dimension of human experience.

A special question of the relation of God's general revelation to reason: the Universals

Since the time of Augustine, Christians have said the human mind is continually illumined by God's mind, as part of his general revelation. This has been called "the light of the mind," "the light of nature," or "the light of reason." Paul said that all people know something about God's "divine nature;" this includes God's majestic holiness as well as many of God's moral attributes, such as love, justice, fairness, honesty, and loyalty. This is the ultimate source of the universals, "The Good," "The True," and "The Beautiful," which people have discussed for centuries. They are known by normal people, perhaps as unacknowledged knowledge, because they are closely related to God's divine nature and attributes, which God continually reveals directly to all people. Even if people cannot recognize the ultimate origin of the universals in the mind of God, yet people can often recognize good actions, true ideas, and matters of beauty on the everyday, non-ultimate level.

An example of a universal, which has been discussed by school teachers for centuries, is "equality," referring to equality in terms of measurement. After a brief explanation, every child seems to know what equality means, whether we are referring to equal distances, equal lengths of time, or equal weights. But where and how did we learn what equality is? In a precise sense, we have never seen, heard, touched, smelled, or tasted equality. We bring an unclarified notion of equality to the use of our normal senses, and most people can begin to clarify what equality is after a short discussion. I think we should say that "Real Equality" exists eternally in the mind of God and that God is continually enlightening the mind of all people, so everyone knows what we mean when we say two distances are equal or two weights are equal. But as soon as we ask where "Real Equality" is, Angst becomes a part of the discussion, because even the most thoughtful person is influenced at this point by his awareness that he deserves to die for his sins.

Another example of the God-given "Light of the Mind" has to do with the way we all trust our five senses to give us real information about our universe. For example, in order for me to be truly certain that my dog is sleeping on the floor near my desk, I have to assume without proof that there is a complex correlation among 1) my senses (I see the dog and hear him snoring.), 2) my cognitive or neurological structures of understanding, and 3) the world that exists outside my senses and reason. Of course, almost all normal people assume these correlations exist, so that I can know that my dog is really sleeping on the floor near me; I would insist that this is a huge but normal leap of faith, meaning faith in the truths we learn by general revelation. Every person lives by faith in truths learned from God's general revelation, but acknowledging the source of these truths raises so much religious Angst that many prefer to avoid the question.

In this way, God's general revelation is a very significant means of his common grace, by which God sustains human life and society. If God's general revelation were to cease, human knowledge would cease, including moral knowledge. I believe humanity would end if God's general revelation did not sustain us; his general revelation is such an organic part of the world we know that the end of general revelation would mean the end of both the world we know and of us as knowers. Paul says that God gives people over to a confused state of mind, but even in that status and situation, people still know many things, including the natural moral law and the universals, which they know only by means of God's general revelation. This knowledge keeps people human, without turning into beasts, even if they dishonor themselves; it is also a preparation for the gospel, which missionaries must use.

D. General Revelation and the Problem of Evil

For centuries we and our parents have asked how God can be both good and all-powerful and still allow good people to suffer so much. This question has resounded throughout modernity and postmodernity with wide-ranging effects. The so-called "Problem of Evil" has been a continuous objection to Christian belief that one encounters in almost every western introduction to philosophy. A classical form of the claim comes from the Scottish philosopher David Hume. He asked, "Is God willing to prevent evil and unable? Then he is not omnipotent. Is he able but not willing? Then he is malevolent. Is he both willing and able? Whence then is evil?"[77] Using arguments like this, many people have needlessly claimed that the existence of real evil in the world makes belief in God impossible or more difficult.

In light of God's general revelation, we see the question has been reversed. People who make the standard claim have not considered deeply

---

[77] This discussion occurs in David Hume's *Dialogues Concerning Natural Religion*, which he finished writing in 1776 and which was published posthumously in 1779. It is available in a variety of editions, and excerpts are included in many anthologies of important texts in western philosophy.

enough what would have to follow if God does not exist; they should spend a day or two reading the fiction of Albert Camus. We have to go deeper than the normal philosophy of religion most of us learned at school.

If God does not exist, we would not be able to say "This is evil" and really mean anything by what we say. For if God does not exist, there is no standard of evaluation to say that something is good or evil; all we could say is that some people like it and others do not like it. A real evaluation that something is evil depends on having a standard that is beyond the opinions of one person or one group of people. Was the Holocaust evil? Hitler and his friends claimed it was good. If you think it was truly evil, you must assume there is a standard outside the differing opinions of people; without thinking about it, you have probably assumed that this standard exists in the mind of God and that the human mind can somehow learn something from the mind of God. Do you think it was truly evil that Stalin caused the deaths of about 100 million people? Stalin and his friends probably claimed it was good. In order to disagree in an intelligent manner, you must think there is a standard of right and wrong beyond mere human disagreements which we can know at least in part. In order to say that 100 million murders is evidence of real evil, we all very naturally assume knowledge of a standard or rule of right and wrong which is above our changing opinions. We all assume a certain amount of moral knowledge which comes from God as part of his moral law built into human consciousness; it is part of being created so that our minds are in the image of God's mind; this is an organic part of God's general revelation. The fact that most normal people can recognize the difference between good and evil and call the actions of a Hitler or Stalin truly evil is, I believe, a strong indicator of the existence of God and the way in which we all use God's natural moral law without further consideration. For me, the "Problem of Evil" is *not* how a good and omnipotent God can allow suffering. For me, the real problem of evil is how a real difference between good and evil could both exist and be recognized by us if God did not exist. Our normal recognition of evil, including the massive human rights movement and the many humanitarian aid organizations dedicated to reducing evil, is possible only because we have significant God-given knowledge of right and wrong.

E. General revelation provides the background for perceiving special revelation and the reality of the Christian Life.

It is the fact of general revelation that makes it possible for people to perceive the authenticity of special revelation and the reality of the Christian life. When Jesus said in John 13:35, "By this everyone will know that you are my disciples, if you love one another," Jesus assumed that everyone is able to recognize love as love. Jesus' teaching about love assumes that people have a God-given understanding of what true love is before they come to faith in the gospel. Everyone has at least a vague knowledge of the character of true love which people receive from God's general revelation which allows people to recognize true love when it is practiced by Christians. It is on the basis of God-given knowledge that "everyone" may evaluate our claims to be disciples of Jesus.

I have claimed that the gospel only comes through special revelation and that there is no gospel in the content of general revelation. But this does not mean there is nothing about love and grace in the content of general revelation. There are significant indications of God's mercy and kindness in his general revelation and common grace, so that his rain falls on the just and the unjust alike. This allows people to recognize special grace as special and to recognize true love when it is practiced.

It is also the fact of general revelation that makes it possible for people to perceive the authenticity of special revelation. Many people read biblical texts which contain penetrating moral depth and immediately perceive the internal authority of the claim. People read Amos 6:8 ("He has showed you, O man, what is good. And what does the Lord require of you? To act justly and to love mercy and to walk humbly with your God."), and they have immediate certainty of the divine authority of the statement. Something similar happens when people read a text like Ephesians 4:29, "Do not let any unwholesome talk come out of your mouths, but only what is helpful for building others up, according to their needs, that it may benefit those who listen." This perception of a deep and proper moral demand in biblical texts of this type occurs because people already have an internal and God-given moral knowledge based on God's natural moral law; matters they previously knew vaguely and partially become explicit with an authority that can hardly be denied. The same is true when people hear, "Do unto others as you would have them do unto you," and "Love your neighbor as yourself," so much that these biblical quotations have often been used as summaries of the natural moral law.

Christians properly ascribe this awareness of the moral authority of biblical moral demands to the testimony of the Holy Spirit; I believe the Holy Spirit connects general revelation with special revelation within this type of human experience. Our ability to perceive the authority of special revelation in moral matters is closely related to the previous general revelation of God's moral law. We should notice the important differences between perceiving the authenticity and authority of the biblical moral law and trusting in the gospel of Christ. I think trusting the gospel is the result of a very special work of the Holy Spirit. But even here I think that believing the gospel is dependent on God's previous general revelation. It is the awareness of what love and grace are, given by general revelation, which allows people to perceive the reality of special grace in the gospel.

F. The Rejection of General Revelation and False Absolutizing

The suppression of general revelation has multiple and extensive effects on academic and educational life. There are many foolish claims of wisdom and knowledge which are the result of darkened hearts, often mixing the claim to know more than one really knows while denying truths we all know because of general revelation. At the center of this problem is false absolutizing. This merits explanation and illustration.

Once people select a particular dimension or aspect of creation as an idol (maybe unconsciously as part of their culture), they commonly interpret all of life, thought, and experience in light of that idol, which leads to a series of idolatrous worldviews and philosophies. A good but partial dimension of God's creation is turned, in the human mind, into a false absolute or replacement for God. For example, the Marxist ideology or philosophy was a result of turning the economic dimension of life into an absolute or idol and then thinking that humans are primarily economic creatures, so that all of life and experience was seen as controlled by economic factors. This philosophy then played a controlling and filtering function in the schools, media, and culture of communist countries, with disastrous results. This deceptive philosophy destroyed the lives of many and has an enduring destructive effect in many parts of the world. However, there was an element of truth in Marxist philosophy; in contrast with some theories before Marx, it correctly noted that socio-economic matters have an important influence on life. This element of truth, which came from general revelation, was falsely absolutized because it was not seen as complementary to other important truths about human life.

The Nazi ideology was the result of turning blood and race into a God-substitute and then interpreting all of life and society in light of this substitute religion. The ideology was then communicated in every possible means in the society under Nazi control, with results so disastrous they need no further mention. But such a demonic ideology had an appeal for many people because it contained an element of truth: that all of us are members of particular peoples, nations, or tribes, a truth recognized even in the Bible. (In the New Testament, there is a strong interest in reconciliation between people groups who were alienated from each other, for example between Jews and Gentiles. The reality of distinct people groups is acknowledged without making any particular group of people an idol.) This presence of a minor truth in the Nazi ideology gave it some power, but because this truth was absolutized and not seen as complementary to other important truths (such as the dignity of all people), it became demonic.

Atheistic existentialism absolutizes human choice or decision, with a marked tendency to think that individual choices or decisions are all that matter in the world, regardless of where those decisions may lead. (Christian and Jewish existentialism are different in important ways.) It has an appeal because of the human desire for individual authenticity which was neglected in some previous worldviews and philosophies. I believe absolutizing the human self in this manner is possible only because of the general revelation of human dignity. But because the dignity of the self is not seen as complementary to other truths and dimensions of creation, the whole philosophy stands in serious tension with the world that God has made and in which we live.

In academic and educational life, one must always ask if the claims one reads are the result of worldviews, ideologies, or philosophies that absolutize one good but partial dimension of creation, making a cognitive idol of a created good, and thereby suppress the general revelation of God. At the same time, one must always be open to find elements of truth which result from general revelation, even within worldviews that are idolatrous.

G. Absolutizing within a Particular Field of Learning

A related effect of the suppression of general revelation in educational and academic life is the tendency for academic theories to falsely absolutize and separate aspects of creation and human experience that properly belong together. Examples can be found in many different academic disciplines, but a selection from the field of ethical theory will be mentioned.

Chapter Eight: Selected Questions in the Philosophy of Religion ...   111

In the common secular (meaning God-denying or God-ignoring) theories about ethics that are not nihilistic (meaning those theories that do not think moral truth is unavailable), there are multiple important and contradictory theories about right and wrong. Most of them claim to be a total explanation of moral life and moral experience. The deontological or Kantian ethicists say that ethics is all about our rational duty in terms of respect for people and universalizable moral laws. The utilitarian ethicists say that ethics is all about the consequences or results of our actions (or moral rules), whether for good or evil, in the lives of other people. The virtue ethics theorists say that ethics is all about what kind of person each of us should become, reaching our potential by means of developing moral character. The social contract ethicists say ethics is all about the formal or informal social agreements that hold society together and prevent social chaos.

From a Christian perspective, one can say that each of these ethical theories contains elements of truth that result from God's general revelation, while each theory also absolutizes one of the ways in which God's natural moral law impacts human consciousness. A proper theistic ethic can include the major elements of each of these moral philosophies within a larger framework coming from the Bible, while also observing that in everyday experience these proper ethical considerations blend or merge together. To repeat: each of these secular ethical theories absolutizes one of the many ways in which God's natural moral law comes to us through creation, without regard for the other complementary ways God's moral comes to us through creation (and also ignoring the Bible). Because unbelief tends to lead to false absolutizing, secular ethical theorists have a tendency to isolate these considerations from each other and to see them as totally contradictory though they can be seen as complementary.

It bears mention that the general revelation of God's moral law is perceived in multiple ways. People often have a direct, intuitive awareness of duties such as love, justice, and loyalty. Rational reflection leads to an awareness of moral laws such as fairness and honesty. And the empirical study of consequences, such as one finds in the social sciences, leads to the recognition of certain moral principles, e.g., that lifetime marriage leads to social, psychological, and economic well-being and that corruption destroys an economy and society. One must see the complementary dimensions in the general revelation of God's moral law, which leads to the several complementary ways in which people perceive his natural moral law.

This brief analysis of the tendency for people to falsely absolutize different aspects of creation in the realm of ethical theory can also be repeated in most fields and disciplines of education and academic life. An understanding of general revelation, and the tendency of people to suppress that revelation, helps us to understand and avoid the problem. Believers must question or criticize this tendency to absolutize parts of creation in education, while we carefully practice a critical discernment that allows us to accept all elements of truth into a biblical worldview that includes the complementarity of truths before God. This effort can help to open the minds of unbelievers to the gospel, while also helping believers to remain faithful to God's truth.

H. Conclusion: Who is wrestling with God's general revelation?

The apostle Paul was a profoundly thoughtful and courageous missionary. He had confidence in the truth and importance of his message in the middle of the various philosophies and multiple religions of his day, and this confidence gave him courage to face manifold problems, whether being shipwrecked, beaten, stoned, or thrown into jail. His missionary courage was rooted in his understanding of the human condition before God, a condition of conflict with God characterized by the rejection and suppression of the knowledge of God which comes from general revelation. It was not Paul who was wrestling with God's general revelation; he saw that all his neighbors across the Mediterranean world of his day were wrestling with God's general revelation.

Believers who live in the global twenty-first century face a world with strong similarities to the world of Paul's time; we face a bewildering variety of secular worldviews, mixed with all sorts of religions. We need missionary courage. God's general revelation and common grace make it possible for people to live like humans, but when we reject God, he may let us go on into a dreadful process of self-punishing self-destruction. Really understanding this condition is the basis for pride in the gospel, the first step in becoming equipped as missionaries.

It is not that we Christians (who must all accept our calling as missionaries) must learn to wrestle with God's general revelation. We should learn more about what God is doing so we can give gratitude to God more appropriately. This is the process of faith seeking understanding, which is the opposite of wrestling against God. We should say "Thank you!" to God regularly for this huge dimension of his common grace. What we need to learn is to see how all our neighbors who do not believe the gospel are wrestling with God's general revelation.

God's self-revelation in Christ was significantly different from what most people expected of a messiah. He was born in a stable or cave, not in a beautiful palace or modern maternity clinic. Though he was presented at the temple as a baby and visited the temple once as a young man, he did not frequent the temple, his Father's house. He grew up in a backwoods village, not the capital city, and he did not attend a prominent school in Jerusalem. He rode a donkey, not a war horse. Perhaps we should say that God's self-revelation in Christ was modest, almost self-deprecating, and a little hidden from view on a global level.

There is, I think, a very important way in which God's self-revelation in creation is also modest. Yes, there is the overwhelming beauty of nature, whether seen in the sky, mountains, the sea, or wonderful plants and animals. But there is also a self-revelation of God that is so much a part of everyday life that we easily fail to notice God's continuous activity. (I am here confessing my own sin.) The important truths we all assume to carry on daily life (regardless of our faith or philosophy of life) are only known because God is revealing them continuously. But it is possible for people to pretend not to notice God's natural revelation; this is partly because of sin and partly because it is so natural, different from what we might expect a revelation from God to be. But people are hiding from God while they wrestle with him and attempt to suppress their knowledge of God. Recognizing the role of God's general revelation in human experience is not only crucial for properly knowing him and giving thanks to him; it also equips us to speak about peace with God among people who are in conflict with God.

If we only read the life of the apostle Paul as recorded in the book of Acts, we might think the key parts of missionary training are learning how to swim in case your ship sinks or learning to sing when you are beaten and thrown into prison. We might think it was tremendously helpful that Paul was able to walk very long distances, or we might be critical of Paul for not learning the local languages of all the people to whom he preached. But when we turn to the book of Romans, Paul's first theme, the foundation of his missionary preparation, was to consider very deeply the conflict with God in which all people are involved. In light of God's general revelation, which, though suppressed, forms the hidden theological assumption of all peoples and cultures, we can see the tremendous importance of the gospel of peace with God. This also takes us an important step forward toward knowing how we understand truth. This provides the courage to enable us to learn the many other things needed to become good missionaries.

Appendices for students of theology and the humanities

Appendix I: The Rejection of General Revelation and the Natural Moral Law in Twentieth-Century Protestant Theology

Karl Barth's influence on the entire Protestant movement in the last century has been very large, especially in regard to considerations of general revelation and God's natural moral law. He led the rejection of natural law and general revelation as normally accepted themes in Protestant theology and ethics during the twentieth century. Most other Protestant thinkers who reject natural law ethics and general revelation as important topics in theology and philosophy are either followers of Barth or have been in some way influenced by the climate of opinion shaped by Barth's thought. This academic question is worthy of serious attention among students of theology and humanities, especially if one is convinced that biblically shaped training for the mission God has entrusted to the church will start by considering God's general revelation very carefully.

1. Karl Barth (1886-1968)

"Human righteousness is, as we have seen, in itself an illusion: there is in this world no observable righteousness. There may, however, be a righteousness before God, a righteousness that comes from Him."[78] With words like these Barth rejected the synthesis of Christianity with European culture and philosophy, a synthesis which he thought went back at least as far as Friedrich Schleiermacher[79] and which, he claimed, led to the religious

---

[78] Karl Barth, *The Epistle to the Romans*, translated from the sixth edition by Edwyn C. Hoskyns (London, Oxford, and NewYork: Oxford University Press, 1933), p. 75.

[79] Friedrich Schleiermacher (1768-1834) is usually described as the "Father of Liberal Theology." He is known for saying that religion is a feeling of absolute dependence; in this way, historic Christian truth claims coming from the Bible and articulated in the creeds were seen as unimportant. In contrast with Schleiermacher, I believe it is crucial for believers to understand that the Christian faith has truth claims at its core.

endorsement of nationalism and militarism.[80] Barth was not so much addressing a single or particular theological issue as much as calling into question a whole pattern of the relation of the Christian faith to western culture, a pattern often called "Culture Protestantism."[81] This pattern reduced Christianity to being the religious component or dimension of the best in the West in such a manner that Christian beliefs were interpreted, evaluated, and accepted in light of or on the basis of ideas coming from western culture. Barth's comments on the thought of Schleiermacher typify his assessment of the whole cultural tradition. According to Schleiermacher, he writes, "The most authentic work of Christianity is making culture the triumph of the Spirit over nature, while being a Christian is the peak of a fully cultured consciousness. The kingdom of God, according to Schleiermacher, is totally and completely identical with the progress of culture."[82] Further, for Schleiermacher, according to Barth, the "existence of churches is really an 'element that is necessary for the development of the human spirit.'"[83] Barth shows his own concerns when, in dialog with Schleiermacher, he suggests that real theologians "should seek the secret of Christianity beyond all culture."[84] Barth's witness is that God stands over against even the best in human culture as both the Judge and Redeemer.

A crucial part of this subordination of Christianity to the best in European culture, claimed Barth, was the doctrine of general revelation and the

---

[80] See Robin W. Lovin, *Christian Faith and Public Choices: The Social Ethics of Barth, Brunner, and Bonhoeffer* (Philadelphia: Fortress Press, 1984), pp. 18-44; and Arthur C. Cochrane, *The Church's Confession Under Hitler* (Philadelphia: Westminster, 1962); Robert P. Ericksen, *Theologians Under Hitler: Gerhard Kittel, Paul Althaus, and Emanuel Hirsch* (New Haven and London: Yale University Press, 1985); and "The Social Philosophy of Karl Barth" by Will Herberg in *Community, State and Church: Three Essays by Karl Barth* edited by Will Herberg (New York: Anchor Books, 1960).

[81] On the general topic of Culture Protestantism see C. J. Curtis, *Contemporary Protestant Thought* (New York: The Bruce Publishing Company, 1970), pp. 97-103. In North America the term "theological liberalism" was often used as a synonym Culture Protestantism in Europe.

[82] "Kultur als Triumph des Geistes ueber die Natur ist das eigenste Werk des Christentums, wie Christlichkeit ihrerseits die Spitze eines durchkultivierten Bewusstseins ist. Das Reich Gottes ist nach Schleiermacher mit dem Fortschritt der Kultur schlechterdings und eindeutig identisch." Karl Barth, *Die protestantische Theologie im 19. Jahrhundert* (Zurich: Evangelischer Verlag, 1946), p. 388.

[83] "Das Bestehen von Kirchen überhaupt 'ein fuer die Entwicklung des menschlichen Geistes notwendiges Element.'" Ibid. p. 396.

[84] "das Geheimnis des Christentums noch jenseits von aller Kulture suchen wollten." Ibid. p. 388.

associated natural theology, the many attempts to prove the existence of God on the basis of reason alone. Though Barth had been speaking out against natural theology for some time before the rise of National Socialism, Hitler's rise to power and the amount of religious support for Hitler brought the issue to a head. "The question became a burning one at the moment when the Evangelical Church in Germany was unambiguously and consistently confronted by a definite and new form of natural theology, namely, by the demand to recognise in the political events of the year 1933, and especially in the form of the God-sent Adolf Hitler, a source of specific new revelation of God, which, demanding obedience and trust, took its place beside the revelation attested in Holy Scripture, claiming it should be acknowledged by Christian proclamation and theology as equally binding and obligatory." This would lead to "the transformation of the Christian Church into the temple of the German nature-and-history-myth."[85]

Barth did not want the immediate crisis of National Socialism to blind Christians to the broader problem of which the church's endorsement of Hitler was, in his opinion, merely a particular manifestation. "The same had already been the case in the developments of the preceding centuries. There can be no doubt that not merely a part but the whole had been intended and claimed when it had been demanded that side by side with its attestation in Jesus Christ and therefore in Holy Scripture the Church should also recognise and proclaim God's revelation in reason, in conscience, in the emotions, in history, in nature and in culture and its achievements and developments."[86] And Barth adds, "If it was admissible and right and perhaps even orthodox to combine the knowability of God in Jesus Christ with His knowability in nature, reason and history, the proclamation of the Gospel with all kinds of other proclamations ... it is hard to see why the German Church should not be allowed to make its own particular use of the procedure."[87]

That is why Barth saw the Barmen Confession (May 31, 1934), of which he was the principle author, as not only a response to the particular problem of the German Christian movement that supported Hitler but also

---

[85] Karl Barth, *Church Dogmatics: A Selection*, Selected with an introduction by Helmut Gollwitzer. Translated and edited by G. W. Bromiley. (New York: Harper and Row, 1962), p. 55. The selection is from CD II,1.
[86] Ibid. On this topic see the excellent treatment in Bruce Demarest, *General Revelation: Historical Views and Contemporary Issues* (Grand Rapids: Zondervan, 1982), pp. 115-134.
[87] Ibid. p. 57.

as an attempt to purify the entire evangelical church of the problem of natural theology. One must read the Barmen Confession as a rejection of natural revelation, natural theology, and a natural law understanding of ethics, which were interpreted as leading to the subordination of Christianity to the best or worst of European culture, when it claims, "Jesus Christ, as He is attested to us in Holy Scripture, is the one Word of God, whom we have to hear and whom we have to trust and obey in life and in death. We condemn the false doctrine that the Church can and must recognise as God's revelation other events and powers, forms and truth, apart from and alongside this one Word of God."[88]

In contrast with any approach that claims to encounter God through natural theology, natural revelation, natural law, or National Socialism, Barth proclaimed that God is known only through his Word, which means only through Christ. Any other approach, he claimed, reduced the Christian faith to a mere religious dimension of western culture.

Barth's approach may be illustrated by his discussion of the traditional Protestant topic of the relation between law and gospel. He thought that sinful humans were very inclined to give the rank and title "law of God" to some demand that does not come from God at all (To repeat, Barth regarded the terrible problem of applying the designation "law of God" to the demands coming from the Nazi movement as representative of a recurring problem.) That is why he strongly recommended changing the traditional phrase "law and gospel" to "gospel and law." "Anyone who really and earnestly would first say Law and only then, presupposing this, say Gospel would not, no matter how good his intention, be speaking of the Law of *God* and therefore then certainly not *his* Gospel."[89] The order "law and gospel," used by Protestants since the Reformation, assumed that there was a revelation of God's law that came through creation which had an impact on human life before people believe the gospel.[90] But this order, Barth thought, left one in danger of giving the title "law of God" to demands that came from the German people or from the Führer or any other source than

---

[88] This is the first article of the Barmen Confession as quoted by Barth, Ibid. p. 54. The entire text of the Barmen Confession appears in Cochrane, op cit. As far as I know, this is the only major Protestant confession that directly denies that God is revealing himself through his creation, though God's general revelation is not discussed at length in some other Protestant confessions.

[89] Karl Barth, "Gospel and Law," as found in *Community, State and Church: Three Essays by Karl Barth* edited and with an introduction by Will Herberg, (New York: Anchor Books, 1960), p. 71.

[90] See Hans O. Tiefel, "The Ethics of Gospel and Law: Aspects of the Barth-Luther Debate." Ph.D. dissertation, Yale University, 1967.

the God and Father of Jesus Christ. To avoid such a travesty, he said, "Gospel and Law," to emphasize that we only know for sure that a law is from God if it follows the gospel. And when he says, "the Law is in the Gospel, from the Gospel and points to the Gospel," it is to make sure everyone knows that "we must first of all know about the Gospel in order to know about the Law, and not vice versa."[91]

To conclude Barth's critique of natural theology/natural law thinking, we should notice one final point. Barth claimed that natural-law thinking robbed people of courage when they had to face and confront evil. "All arguments based on natural law are Janus-headed. They do not lead to the light of clear decisions, but to misty twilight in which all cats become gray. They lead to—Munich."[92] Barth's great courage in resisting the Nazis, as he saw it, arose from his starting point in hearing the revelation of God in Jesus Christ. He thought any other basis for ethics, whether natural law or any other method, led to moral compromise.

2. Helmut Thielicke (1908-1986)

Helmut Thielicke's rejection of natural law broadly follows Karl Barth, who was one of Thielicke's first theology professors in Bonn in the early thirties. (Thielicke was also involved in the anti-Nazi movement among Protestant Christians in Germany during World War II.) Nevertheless, Thielicke added a number of considerations that are worthy of separate discussion. Starting with his biblical exegesis, whereas traditionally Protestants had associated the Ten Commandments with the natural moral law, Thielicke associated the Ten Commandments with "natural lawlessness."[93] Noting the negative structure of most of the commandments

---

[91] Barth, "Gospel and Law," p. 72. I have responded to Barth's views on law and gospel in"Law and Gospel: The Hermeneutical/Homiletical Key to Reformation Theology and Ethics," *Evangelical Review of Theology*, vol. 36, no 2, April 2012.

[92] Barth as quoted in Herberg, ed. p. 49. The reference to "Munich" is to the Munich Agreement of 1938 in which France and Britain permitted the Nazi takeover of the part of Czechoslovakia called the "Sudentenland." It became a watchword for the futile appeasement of totalitarianism.

[93] Helmut Thielicke, *Theological Ethics: Volume 1: Foundations*, edited and translated by William H. Lazareth (Grand Rapids: Eerdmans, reprint edition, 1984; copyright Fortress Press, 1966), p. 444. The material about Thielicke is broadly dependent on Thomas K. Johnson, "Helmut Thielicke's Ethics of Law and Gospel," Ph.D. dissertation, University of Iowa, 1987. As an example of the traditional Protestant view, John Calvin claimed natural law, "which we have above described as written, even engraved, upon the hearts of all, in a sense asserts the very

("Thou shalt not ..."), he claims, "There is within this negativity a protest against man as he actually is."[94] This is the opposite, he claimed, of the assumptions that inform natural law theories. "The order of being presupposed in all conceptions of natural law can be assumed only on the presupposition that the fall has only a comparatively accidental but not an essential significance."[95] "Natural law and the Decalogue in fact belong to completely different worlds."[96] Rather than connecting with a natural law within human nature, Thielicke claimed, the Ten Commandments harshly confront and condemn our natural lawlessness.

This relates closely to the problems Thielicke saw within Culture Protestantism. Whereas "The Decalogue is expressly set down within the context of a dialogue"[97] meaning a dialogue with God in personal faith, natural law and Culture Protestant ethics, he claimed, conceive of moral decisions as being made by solitary egos, seeing God as merely the distant author of moral laws.

> Culture Protestantism makes Christianity into a form of the world (*Weltgestalt*) in the sense that the commands of God—including the command to love one's neighbor—are detached from the divine *auctor legis* and from the relationship of decision and faith with this author. One could also say that Culture Protestantism tends to separate the second table of the law from the first Commandment ("I am the Lord your God; you shall have no other gods besides me.") and then represents the individual commandments as maxims of Christian behavior.[98]

Thielicke thought that as soon as the commands of God are separated from their source, they undergo a change of meaning that leaves them significantly different from what they were intended to be. Specifically, biblical moral prescriptions are easily subjected to ideological perversion once they are separated from God. For example, Thielicke thought the maxim "Gemeinnutz geht vor Eigennutz" ("The interests of the group come before the interests of the individual.") is a possibly legitimate application of the bib-

---

same things that are to be learned from the two Tables." *Institutes of the Christian Religion*, ed. John T. McNeill, trans. Ford Lewis Battles (Philadelphia: The Westminster Press, 1960), II.vii.1. This same connection of God's natural moral law with the Ten Commandments is present in most of the Protestant Reformers.

[94] Ibid. p. 441.
[95] Ibid. p. 443.
[96] Ibid. p. 444.
[97] Ibid. p. 442.
[98] Helmut Thielicke, *Kirche und Öffentllichkeit: Zur Grundlegung einer lutherischen Kulturethik* (Tuebingen: Furche Verlag, 1947), p. 44.

lical love command. But it was used by the Nazis to support their program that was initially called "Christianity of Action" and was later called "Socialism of Action," so that the application of a proper biblical principle was controlled and misdirected by a terrible ideology. Thielicke also saw in the early works of Karl Marx a secularized form of expression of Christian love, but once this love command was separated from its Source and integrated into the system of historical materialism, the meaning of the command was substantially changed.[99] Any moral theory that allows any independence of a moral command from God risks serious ideological perversion. "Only the one who stands in personal contact with the Lord of the First Commandment, as one who has been called and who follows, recognizes that the commands of God are something 'wholly other.'"[100]

Thielicke not only took this new direction in interpreting the Ten Commandments; he also took a new direction in interpreting the Sermon on the Mount that corresponds with his rejection of natural law ethics.

> The harsh and apparently alien aspect of the Sermon on the Mount is its true point. It makes its demands with no regard for constitutional factors such as the impulses or for the limitations imposed on my personal will by autonomous structures ... It does not claim me merely in a sphere of personal freedom. It thus compels me to identify myself with my total I. Hence I have to see in the world, not merely the creation of God, but also the structural form of human sin, i.e., its suprapersonal form, the "fallen" world ... I have to confess that I myself have fallen, and that what I see out there is the structural objectification of my fall.[101]

Whereas Culture Protestants, natural law theorists, and "German Christians" generally saw societal structures as the result of creation, perhaps calling them "creation orders," Thielicke saw them as resulting from the Fall. Other views, he claimed, resulted from minimizing the total demand of God encountered in the Sermon on the Mount and left people without a complete sense of responsibility for all their actions.

This also corresponds with Thielicke's discussion of the problem of "autonomous norms" (*Eigengesetzlichkeit* in German). To appreciate Thielicke's comments one must keep in mind Barth's concern that people

---

[99] Helmut Thielicke, *Vernunft und Existenz bei Lessing: Das Unbedingte in der Geschichte* (Goettingen: Vandenhoeck & Ruprecht, 1981), p. 49.
[100] *Kulturethik*, pp. 45,46.
[101] Helmut Thielicke, *The Evangelical Faith: Volume Two: The Doctrine of God and of Christ*, translated and edited by Goeffrey W. Bromiley (Grand Rapids: Eerdmans, 1977), p. 248.

tend to call a law "the law of God" or otherwise grant moral authority to a norm that it absolutely should not have.

> Since Kant the fact is known and deeply rooted in our thinking that the individual spheres of life are endowed with their autonomous norms (*Eigengesetzlichkeit*). He imputed this autonomous structure principally to the spheres of meaning (*Sinngebiete*) of the ethical, the esthetical and the theoretical. More recently one has learned to reckon with the autonomy of all the historical spheres of life; one knows of the autonomy of the state, of economic life, of law and of politics. One grants each of these historical spheres an autonomous structure because it is endowed with a constituting principle, from which all its proper functions can be derived.[102]

Because people think there are "immanent principles which so control the processes involved as to make them proceed automatically,"[103] people tend to say business is business, art is art, politics is politics. People talk and act as if there is some kind of natural law or law of nature in each sphere of society that has its own validity and authority regardless of any moral principles or ethical rules. But rather than falsely seeing these autonomous norms, whether in business, art, politics, or another sphere of life as coming from God, Thielicke sees these norms as the expression of our fallenness. They are structural expressions of sin, not creation orders in which we encounter a God-given natural moral law.[104] And if one of these immanent principles or autonomous norms is absolutized, turned into an idol, the great secular ideologies like National Socialism or Communism tend to arise.[105]

Thielicke claimed that all natural law theories of ethics made two crucial assumptions: 1. There is a perceptible order of being or structure of the world that can be traced back to creation. 2. Human reason is largely un-

---

[102] Helmut Thielicke, *Geschichte und Existenz: Grundlegung einer evangelischen Geschichtstheologie* (Gütersloh: Verlag C. Bertelsmann, 1935), p. 46.

[103] TE, 2, p. 71.

[104] Here Thielicke was especially thinking of the problem that some of the Nazi-oriented "German Christians" said that the law of God comes through the Nazi "VolK" as a creation order, so that the law of the Nazi Volk can be called the law of God.

[105] TE, 2, p. 72. There is a very similar discussion of the topic of autonomous norms in the work of the Danish thinker N. H. Soe. See his *Christliche Ethik* (München: Chr. Kaiser Verlag, 1957). The similarity of the two discussions by two thinkers who were both deeply influenced by Karl Barth suggests that this type of assessment of societal structures flows from the basic lines of Barth's theology.

touched by sin so that this moral order can be perceived by all people.[106] From the preceding discussion it should be clear that Thielicke did not think the current structure of our world could be traced back to creation. In addition it should be noted that Thielicke claimed human reason is not able to discern the good without revelation. Human reason is so distorted by sin that it is the expression of human fallenness and therefore unable to ethically evaluate fallen humanity.[107]

Thielicke thought that Protestant ethics needed to go through a process of purification similar to the purification of Protestant theology that occurred during the Reformation. This means purifying Protestant ethics of any notion of natural law as an analogy to purifying Protestant theology of salvation by works. "Man's incapacity to justify himself by good works is logically to be augmented by, or integrated with, a similar incapacity truly to know the will and commandment of God."[108] All Protestant ethics should be only an ethics of justification by faith alone. This leaves no place at all for any notion of natural law or an ethics of general revelation.

3. H. Evan Runner (1916-2002)

H. Evan Runner was a North American follower of the "Philosophy of the Cosmonomic Idea," crafted by the Dutch Protestant thinker Herman Dooyeweerd (1894-1977). While this movement was not under direct influence from Barth or Thielicke, it has important similarities. Like Barth, the followers of Dooyeweerd are generally very critical of the medieval synthesis of the biblical and classical traditions, thinking this synthesis led to the secularization of Europe and North America. And like Barth, this movement is very critical of any synthesis of Christian beliefs with Enlightenment or post-Enlightenment European culture.

In a speech delivered in 1957 in Calgary, Alberta, Canada, Runner argued vehemently that modern Christians should completely reject natural law theory.[109] Runner thought we should trace the origins of modern natu-

---

[106] TE, 1, p. 388.
[107] Helmut Thielicke, *Theologische Ethik*, Band II,1: *Entfaltung* 1. Teil: *Mensch und Welt* (Tübingen: J. C. B. Mohr, 1955), pp. 371-383. Unfortunately his "Theological Critique of Reason" does not appear in the English edition.
[108] TE 1, p. 326. What Thielicke says on this topic can be seen as a development of related themes in Barth's writings. See Barth, "No!" in *Natural Theology*, p. 97.
[109] "The Development of Calvinism in North America on the Background of Its Development in Europe." As far as I know, this valuable lecture was never published. Its importance is shown by its presence in an informal format in various libraries. Illness may have prevented Runner from completing the project.

ral law theory to the deist philosophy of Lord Herbert of Cherbury (1583-1648), especially seen in his book *De Veritate* (1624). In an age of raging conflict that was devastating Europe (the Thirty Years War, 1618-1648), Herbert advocated a "universal" religion and a "universal" law that could overcome the conflicts between men. Obviously this deprives Christianity of distinctiveness, which Runner thought is clearly wrong.

Just a year later came Hugo Grotius's *De Jure belli et pacis* (1625). According to Runner's interpretation, Grotius sharply distinguishes the Law of God from the Law of Nature. And though Grotius believed in the Law of God, he thought the foundation of public life in Europe should be the Law of Nature, not the Law of God. These ideas were further developed a generation later by Samuel Pufendorf, who also sharply distinguished the plane of divine revelation from the plane of natural law. And thus, argues Runner, a whole new outlook developed that was contrary to the Reformation faith. Man is no longer seen as a covenantal being whose meaning is found in relation to God. Man is now seen as a rational-moral being who has within himself a proper guide to life and the ability to act according to this guide. Though "Such men did not hesitate to leave Revelation and the Kingdom of Christ to the private lives of those who showed some concern for these matters," yet "These were the men who took up with unfailing confidence the building of the Kingdom of Man on Earth. Communism is one form of the general pattern."[110]

In this way Runner thinks the medieval dualistic scheme of Nature/Grace came back into Protestant lands with disastrous results. The medieval synthesis, he thinks, was really an attempt to hold on to pagan philosophy in the realm of Nature while adding Christian beliefs in the restricted realm of Grace or Supernature. Runner and the other thinkers in his movement are critical of the Protestant Reformers for not more completely replacing the medieval Nature/Grace framework with what they would regard as a more authentic evangelical philosophy. As he reads Christian history, because the Reformers failed in this important task, the Nature/Grace framework came back into Protestant thought and culture shortly after the Reformation. The theology of Phillip Melanchthon (1497-1560, colleague of Martin Luther at the University of Wittenberg) already shows terrible signs of this trend. The Nature/Grace framework of thought made Revelation and the Christian faith irrelevant to the important areas of law, politics, and business, in this way contributing to the secularization of western culture. Natural law theories, whether Protestant or Catholic, are an important part of Nature/Grace dualism. Therefore, argues Runner, Reformed Chris-

---

[110] Runner, p. 8.

tians should reject any theory of natural law as part of rejecting Nature/Grace dualism and secularization.

4. Responses

Coming from Barth, Thielicke, and Runner, we encounter three very serious types of reasons for rejecting general revelation and especially the natural moral law as standard and important themes in Protestant theology and ethics. For Barth, consideration of the natural moral law and general revelation is part of the natural theology that reduced the Christian faith to the religious dimension of western culture and lost sight of the otherness of God; natural theology was part of the distinctive religious-cultural synthesis of Culture Protestantism in which ideas from the secular Enlightenment overruled truly Christian convictions so that Christians and the church were not able to stand against society as prophetic critics. Following Barth's claim that theological theories about general revelation and the natural moral law are part of subordinating the Christian faith to secular culture, Thielicke claims that human life is largely structured by sin, and human reason is so heavily shaped by sin that reason cannot derive any reliable moral norms from the structure of human life. In a slightly different line, Runner rejects any supposedly Christian theory of a natural moral law because it is a part of the Nature/Grace dualism that contributed to the destructive secularization of western civilization.

The rejection of any theory of the natural moral law, often joined with a minimized understanding of the role of God's general revelation in human life and culture, has several negative effects on the pattern of life within the Christian church and on our overall understanding of the mission God has given to the church. It can blind us to the way in which our neighbors are already wrestling with God and are in conflict with God. We may miss the way in which the biblical message addresses the primordial Ängste and deepest questions which our neighbors face. It leaves the impression that our non-Christian neighbors can have no knowledge of right and wrong, unless that knowledge is derived from Christ or the Bible. And it can point our eyes (and our unbelieving neighbors' eyes) away from seeing God's active role in maintaining his creation (common grace) by means of his continuing word in creation (general revelation), which together set the conditions for God's call to repent and believe the gospel. This weakened set of theological/philosophical convictions can easily distort the relation to society and culture of individual Christians and the entire church community. Rather than understanding and embracing the way in which God has sent the entire church (and every member of the church) into society as carriers of the gospel of peace with God, a denial of God's general revelation and natural moral law pushes Christians toward a fight-or-flight relation to society. If we think that God is not already active in our world in his general revelation and common grace, we often end up with either an "ethics of holy community," the flight relation to society which assumes we can and must purify ourselves from sin by limited contact with the world, or an "ethics of domination," the fight relation to society which assumes we must impose God's law on our neighbors because they know nothing about right and wrong, thereby initiating their conflict with God. Both moral/religious stances toward society hinder proper missions and result from a minimized understanding or denial of God's general revelation.[111]

Though our studies in Romans 1:18-2:5 are already a response to Barth, Thielicke, and Runner and were written in light of their concerns, some additional comments are in order. Obviously, as evangelical Christians our first priority is to discover how a theme is presented in the Bible, following which we must evaluate theological and philosophical theories in light of biblical teaching. It is completely clear that the apostle Paul preached the gospel of Christ in light of God's previous word through creation and that Paul's teaching fits organically with similar themes in the rest of the Bible.

In response to Evan Runner: it seems to me that the type of classical Christian natural law theories one sees in Thomas Aquinas, Martin Luther, and John Calvin is substantially different from the early Enlightenment theories found in Grotius and Pufendorf. It seems very likely that Grotius and Pufendorf put natural law theory within a dualistic (therefore secularizing) framework, but that Aquinas, Luther, and Calvin used natural law theory without this dualism, even if a limited grace/nature dualism may be seen in some of the writings of Aquinas. I believe that classical Protestant natural law theories as seen in Luther and Calvin formed an organic part of their doctrines of creation and general revelation that tend to overcome dualistic tendencies within the Christian community. And what the apostle

---

[111] In other places I have described a more holistic understanding of the relation between faith and culture. I believe that the proper concerns represented by the "ethics of holy community" can better be described under the motive of the "construction" of new cultural forms within the Christian community, while the proper concerns represented by the "ethics of domination," can better be described under the motive of the "contribution" of cultural entities from the Christian community to our various cultures. The motives of cultural construction and contributions to culture should be completed by the motives of the prophetic critique of cultures and the correlation of the gospel with the questions and Ängste present in a culture. For more, see Thomas K. Johnson, "Christ and Culture," *Evangelical Review of Theology*, 35:1, January, 2011.

Paul said about God's general revelation and natural moral law was part of his missionary response to his situation that was alternately secular or filled with a vast array of different religions.

In response to Helmut Thielicke: The understanding of the natural moral law which I have learned from Paul's epistle to the Romans does not assume that reason is sinless but rather that the general revelation of God's moral law is the key element that makes moral reason and civilization itself possible, even when our moral reason may be defending itself against God's demand. God's natural moral law and general revelation stand in constant tension with human natural (natural in the sense of coming from sin, not natural in the sense of resulting from creation) lawlessness. And what we see in Romans suggests that the structural expression of sin assumes a deeper structure of life given in creation (and a general revelation of that creation order) that still exists, even if sin means it exists in a distorted manner. And did not Thielicke assume, contrary to his own claims, that the confrontation of our natural lawlessness by the law of God in Scripture is possible because people have a previously given (perhaps vague) idea that murder, stealing, and lying are wrong?

In response to Karl Barth's courageous confrontation of the moral and theological weakness of Culture Protestantism, some questions must also be raised. Is it possible that Barth's grasp of the otherness of God and the need for revelation from on high could be better served by a different kind of critique of his religious/cultural situation? Could one not better use a transcendental critique of unbelief (which assumes God's active and ongoing general revelation) and an analysis of the wrath of God such as offered in the earlier chapters of this book? My critique of Culture Protestantism would be different from Barth's critique.

I believe that a continual synthesis of Christianity with philosophy and culture is not only a human necessity, based on the need of the intellectually mature and authentic Christian to overcome spiritual schizophrenia and have a unified faith and worldview. A synthesis of our Christian faith with culture and learning is also highly desirable because we should want to worship God with the entirety of our lives. And a significant interaction between our Christian truth claims and the truth claims of a culture or cultures becomes an obvious need as soon as we take up the missionary calling God has given to the church. But the crucial question faced by Christians in all ages and cultures is the role of our Christian truth claims in relation to the role of the ideas and values from our cultures in our total religious-cultural synthesis or worldview. (My analysis of this problem is dependent on Helmut Thielicke's methodological contrast of "Cartesian

Theology" with "Non-Cartesian Theology" to show the problems of Culture Protestantism and similar movements,[112] as well as on H. Richard Niebuhr's terminology "Christ of Culture,"[113] which is also addressing this problem.) Phrased in ideal terms, there are two primary intellectual alternatives faced by each individual Christian and by every Christian community: either our central Christian beliefs function as control beliefs and cognitive filters that determine which of the beliefs and values from our cultures we accept, *or*, the beliefs and values of our cultures serve as control beliefs and cognitive filters that determine which Christian beliefs we accept and how we interpret them. In generalized terms and recognizing the complexity of the movement, Culture Protestantism evaluated, appropriated, and interpreted the Christian faith using the control beliefs and cognitive filters provided by the European Enlightenment and the following rationalist and romantic movements. As a result, important themes in Christian theology and ethics were filtered out, meaning they were not mentioned or not believed. What should have been occurring in the churches is that pastors and individual Christians would be evaluating and selectively accepting or rejecting the ideas and values of the Enlightenment (and the following cultural movements) on the basis of and in light of central Christian convictions such as have been summarized in the Christian creeds. (I am thinking especially of the Apostles' Creed and the Nicene Creed.) Overall, Culture Protestantism neglected or denied the holiness and wrath of God, the universal validity and objectivity of God's moral law, and the depths of human sin, with a result that the incarnation, crucifixion, and resurrection were not seen as extremely important. To emphasize one point, most of the leading theologians of the entire Culture Protestant movement denied an objective or absolute moral law coming from God, regardless of whether God communicated this moral law through creation (as the natural moral law) or through Scripture (as biblical ethics), because their previously accepted control beliefs arising from Enlightenment philosophy filtered out belief in an objective moral law. Core Christian convictions, both about the moral law and about the gospel, were filtered out because pastors, theologians, and church members were evaluating and appropriating the biblical message using the ideas and values of the Enlightenment. If these Christians had used the opposite method, the religious and cultural results would

---

[112] See Helmut Thielicke, *The Evangelical Faith: Vol. 1: Prolegomena: The Relation of Theology to Modern Thought Forms*, translated and edited by Geoffrey W. Bromiley (Grand Rapids: William B. Eerdmans, 1974), 420 pages.

[113] See H. Richard Niebuhr's classic analysis in *Christ and Culture* (New York: Harper & Row, 1951), 259 pages.

have been quite different; perhaps the humanitarian disasters of World War II and the Holocaust could have been prevented.[114]

Karl Barth and Helmut Thielicke were surely right to reject the total theological/cultural worldview of Culture Protestantism. Evan Runner was surely right to reject the views regarding the natural moral law that contributed to the secular Enlightenment in the seventeenth and eighteenth centuries. But rather than Christians rejecting the themes of God's general revelation and his natural moral law from our theology and ethics, we should see that all of unbelieving life, thought, and culture is involved in suppressing the unavoidable knowledge from God and about God which God is proclaiming through his creation. Then we will be more equipped to also proclaim the gospel of God which is revealed in Scripture.[115]

---

[114] This "opposite method" of evaluating the ideas and values of our multiple cultures in light of our core Christian convictions always involves multiple steps which I have described as the multiple proper interactions between the Christian faith and culture. There were multiple valuable convictions and intellectual apprehensions which came to light in Enlightenment thought which Christians can accept if they are accepted through the filter of orthodox Christian beliefs.

[115] An example of a twenty-first century European theologian who is consciously moving in the opposite direction than Barth and Thielicke is Pavel Hošek. See his important essay, "The Christian claim for universal human rights in relation to natural law," *International Journal for Religious Freedom*, 5:2, 2012, pp. 147-160.

Appendix II: Types of Beliefs

In this book I have made reference to different types of beliefs that people hold, using terms such as "professed beliefs," "practiced beliefs," and "control beliefs." These distinctions merit further comment. As I am using these terms, they refer to the different roles and functions a belief can have within the human mind, assuming there is such an entity as a cognitive structure or a blueprint of the human mind. The way I am using these terms may be different from how these terms are used in some branches of psychology and philosophy.

I use the term "professed beliefs" to refer to all the ideas and convictions that a person is conscious of believing and about which this person is able to say, "I believe ..." or "I am convinced of ..." These professed beliefs may be either rather trivial (e.g., The lamp on my desk is on right now.) or truly profound (e.g., I believe that God is Triune.).

I use the term "practiced beliefs" to refer to all the ideas and convictions that shape a person's behavior, whether or not the person is conscious that a belief is playing this role in life. A practiced belief may stand in conflict with a professed belief. For example, a person may deny being a racist or even deny that the word "race" refers to any definable entity (my point of view) but then treat people with a different skin tone as superior or inferior. Or, as mentioned in a previous chapter of this book, a person may claim to be a moral relativist and then go on to make good use of God's natural moral law. The truths that all people know as a result of God's general revelation (but often suppress from consciousness) are often practiced, perhaps in a negative manner, while not being professed. We can also refer to these truths known via God's general revelation, even if denied, as the "transcendental conditions of human experience."

I use the terms "control beliefs" and "filter beliefs" synonymously to refer to those beliefs that play an authoritative role in a person's mind either to rule in or to rule out other professed beliefs. Control beliefs play a role in the human mind that is similar to the role of a referee in a sporting event. For example, for many university students I have taught, atheistic evolutionary theory has played the role of a control belief or filter belief. As a result of this control belief, they have not been able to profess to believe in an objective moral law and have had great difficulty explaining what makes humans different from animals; atheistic evolutionary theory has filtered out professing belief in truths that they have known as a result of God's general revelation, pushing these generally revealed truths into a

Appendix II: Types of Beliefs

suppressed status in their minds. As a referee in the mind, atheistic evolutionary theory says a person may not admit to believing there is an absolute moral law.

It is my personal observation that such control or filter beliefs usually address three types of themes: what really and ultimately exists; how we should interpret our experiences of guilt, shame, and forgiveness; and what is the big story of history. Therefore, very generally, worldviews and religions have three intellectual structures (which function as control beliefs or cognitive filters), thereby shaping all that people believe: an ontological structure, which describes what ultimately exists; an existential structure, which describes our experiences of guilt, duty, and forgiveness; and a historical structure, which describes the flow of history. As Christians we also have three intellectual structures that outline our entire faith and philosophy of life. Our Christian ontological structure is oriented around our doctrine of the Trinity; our existential structure or control belief is oriented around the relation between law and gospel; and our historical structure is the biblical meta-story of creation, fall, redemption, and final restoration. We should consciously use these core Christian convictions as our control beliefs and cognitive filters. Part of the authenticity and holism of being a Christian is that my professed beliefs, my practiced beliefs, and my filter beliefs can be completely unified and reconciled when I recite the Apostle's Creed or the Nicene Creed in worship of God along with fellow Christians.

Appendix III: The Missions Training Structure of the Epistle to the Romans

Thomas Schirrmacher has kindly provided the following chart of the structure of Paul's Epistle to the Romans, which documents and clarifies the way in which Paul's teaching is framed by his missionary purposes. It is this mission-oriented structure of Paul's teaching which pushes us to conclude that studying the book of Romans can constructively shape missions training today.[116]

\multicolumn{3}{c}{On the Framework of the Letter to the Romans:}		
\multicolumn{3}{c}{Parallels between Romans 1:1-15 and 15:14-16:27}		
1:1-6	The gospel was foretold in the Old Testament.	16:25-27
1:5	The obedience that comes from faith has to be proclaimed to all nations.	16:26; 15:18
1:7	Grace and peace to you …	16:20
1:8	The faith of the Roman Christians is known throughout the whole world.	16:19
1:8-13	Paul plans to travel to Rome via Jerusalem.	15:22-29
1:11-12	Paul seeks to be spiritually encouraged by the Christians in Rome.	15:24
1:13	In spite of his wishes, Paul has been prevented from traveling to Rome up to this time.	15:22
1:13-15	The gospel has to be proclaimed to all peoples.	15:14-29; comp. 16:26

---

[116] This chart is from Thomas Schirrmacher, "The Book of Romans as a Charter for World Missions: Why mission and theology have to go together," a gift from the Theological Commission to the Missions Commission of the World Evangelical Alliance, distributed at the meeting of the Missions Commission, November 7, 2011.

Questions for study and discussion

Introduction

1. Compare the introduction to Romans (1:1-15) with the conclusion (15:14-16:27). Why do you agree or disagree with the claim that the whole epistle is designed for missions training?

2. Compare this translation with the translation in your Bible. What fine nuances are different? How do these nuances influence your understanding of God and people?

3. How do you know the gospel of Christ is true? How do you know that God is real? Why should we not believe in many gods?

4. What will equip you to comfortably explain the Christian message to:
   a. People who claim to be atheists?
   b. People who think we cannot know truth?
   c. People who think we all find or create our own truth?
   d. People who follow another religion?
   e. People who substitute morality for faith?
   f. People who may be much more educated than you?
   g. People who are less educated than you?

5. Do you feel uncomfortable when you talk about your beliefs or your ethics with people who think entirely differently from you? Why?

6. Who needs an "apology," a defense of his/her beliefs?

7. In what ways is being a Christian an education in itself?

Chapter One: The Human Condition, pages 17ff

1. What is the central self-contradiction within human life? How do you experience this and also see it in the lives of others?

2. In what way does everyone know God? In what way do some not know God?

3. What contents does everyone know because of general revelation? How is this different from how you have previously thought about general revelation?

4. How does each of the seven content areas of general revelation form or provide a needed condition for human life and experience? How is culture dependent on general revelation?

5. What are the advantages and disadvantages of each term: general revelation, natural revelation, and creational revelation?

6. Describe epistemological injustice. Give examples from everyday life.

7. What is the difference between professed belief and practiced belief? Why are people commonly of two minds, living and thinking in tension with their professed beliefs?

8. Describe religious reversals and substitute religions in your experience or your community.

9. How do Isaiah chapters 44 and 46 form the background for Romans 1?

10. Why is everyone religious? In what creator and redeemer might you believe if you were not a Christian?

Chapter Two: The Human Condition, part 2, pages 31ff

1. To what does God "give people over?"

2. How is Paul's description of the wrath of God in this text different from other descriptions of God's wrath you have heard? What complementary descriptions of God's wrath are found in the Bible?

3. How can sin be self-punishing?

4. In what ways are the sins listed in verses 29 to 31 self-destructive or self-dishonoring?

5. Read Jeremiah 2 and compare it with Romans 1. What are the similarities and differences?

6. Why do biblical writers such as Amos and Paul tell people about God's law when they assume people already know about God's law?

7. What would it look like to imitate Amos 1 today?

8. What does the process of mutual moral evaluation tell us about ourselves and the universe? What is the totally illogical part of this process?

9. What questions will help unbelievers to acknowledge to themselves what they already know about God's wrath and God's common grace?

Interlude on Contemporary Theology, pages 45ff

1. Has your previous understanding of God's general revelation been distorted? Was that distortion similar to one of the distortions briefly described?

2. Have you perceived distorted or one-sided approaches to God's two revelations, general and special, in your Christian circles? What can you do to move toward a more balanced and complete perspective?

3. When you think about "what God is doing," do you think mostly about what God is doing by means of his general revelation or by means of his special revelation? Is something lacking in your knowledge of God?

4. Try to describe the ways in which the distorted understandings of general revelation, which were briefly described, would influence or distort our approach to the mission God has given to believers in the great commission.

5. How would distorted understandings of God's general revelation influence our efforts as Christians in politics, business, and education? What influence would such distortions have on our approach to marriage, family, and parenting?

Chapter Three: Angst and General Revelation, pages 53ff

1. What is "philosophy?" How is philosophy different from but related to religion and theology?

2. How is Christian philosophy related to biblical statements such as "The fear of the Lord is the beginning of knowledge" (Proverbs 1:7) and "be transformed by the renewing of your mind" (Romans 12:2)?

3. What is the relation between general revelation and Angst?

4. What is the relation between special revelation and Angst?

5. Can you identify a word that is better than the word Angst to describe this type of human experience?

6. What type or types of Angst are predominant in your life or in your culture? How does your individual or culturally predominant variety of Angst influence the experience of other varieties of Angst?

7. How does the Bible correlate with your Angst?

8. Can you identify a better word than the word correlation to describe the relation between Angst and the promises of God in the Bible?

9. How do the people who need to hear the gospel from you experience Angst? How does the Bible relate to their needs?

Chapter Four: Moral Angst, pages 63ff

1. Why do people experience moral Angst?

2. How are experiences such as shame and social rejection related to moral Angst?

3. What is the relation between Angst and the many historical religious and cultural traditions?

4. What role does guilt play in your life and in the lives of your neighbors?

5. How have you responded to moral Angst?

6. How are many of your neighbors responding to moral Angst?

7. What is the role of guilt in the lives of the people who need to hear the gospel from you?

8. On what basis can we distinguish true guilt from false guilt?

9. Why do people try to cleanse themselves from guilt and shame?

10. How do people try to cleanse themselves from guilt and shame?

Chapter Five: Existential Angst, pages 67ff

1. Why did Camus and Russell find life to be meaningless?

2. Why did Ecclesiastes find life to be meaningless?

3. In order for your life or my life to have meaning, does the entire universe need to have a meaning or direction?

4. Why might some people not want to talk about the meaning of life?

5. What is the relation between suicide and meaninglessness?

6. What is the relation between boredom and meaninglessness?

7. What is the relationship between entertainment and the search for meaning?

8. In what ways does the telling of stories and legends relate to the human need for meaning?

9. In what way does meaning contribute to courage and joy?

10. How do personal relationships relate to our need for meaning?

11. How does knowing God influence the meaning of daily work and relationships?

12. How are our neighbors wrestling with meaninglessness? How does the Christian message answer their need?

Chapter Six: Ontological Angst, pages 73ff

1. Why are some people afraid of death?

2. What role does the fear of death play in life?

3. How is the fear of death related to other varieties of Angst?

4. What role does fear of the future (secondary ontological Angst) play in the life of your society? In the lives of your neighbors? In your life?

5. What is "naked faith?" How is it different from a combination of faith and reason?

6. What is "religious panic?" What roles might it play in the lives of individuals and societies?

7. How do you respond to religious panic?

8. What steps do people normally take to respond to fear of the future? How does an authentic faith influence such normal steps regarding fear of the future?

9. How do the promises of God in the Bible relate to ontological Angst?

10. How can we best talk about God's promises in relation to the ontological Angst of our neighbors who need those promises?

Chapter Seven: General Revelation and the Human Quest, pages 79ff

1. What are the similarities between the Bloodhound Gang and the Buddha?

2. What the most common answers to the human quest in your community or culture? How are they competing for the loyalty of adherents?

3. What is the relation between the questions (and quest) that arise from human existence and historical narratives? How is this both similar to and different from the relation between Angst and history?

4. How has globalization influenced the process of the human quest? How should the globalization of the human quest inform our approach to missions and the education of people who grow up within a Christian church?

5. What are the advantages and disadvantages of distinguishing between Angst and the human quest? Should the two themes be merged together?

6. When should we quickly give biblical answers to the questions that people ask? When should we decide to let people wrestle with their questions (and continue wrestling with God)?

7. Why do people seem not to fully believe their own beliefs? Why is there such a pronounced tension between professed beliefs and practiced beliefs for so many people?

8. Look at each of the ten questions listed above. With each question describe the extent to which the question is already answered by God's general revelation and the extent to which the question is only answered by God's special revelation in the Bible.

9. What questions would you add to this list of ten questions? Why?

Chapter Eight: Selected Questions in the Philosophy of Religion in Light of God's General Revelation, pages 97ff

1. Why do religions frequently have themes and rituals that replace biblical themes and rituals? Can you think of more examples than were given in the text? What other replacements have you observed for Christian beliefs in creation, redemption, and revelation?

2. Should we prove the existence of God? Why? Why not? What are the risks involved in proving God's existence? What are the advantages to Christians of proving the existence of God? In what way is a proof for God an attack on the spiritual defenses of our neighbors?

3. In what way is God's general revelation the condition that makes human reason possible? How do you know you can trust your five

senses? What is God's role in the fact that you know what equality measurement is?

4. How have you heard the question of the problem of evil? Was the question more a request for companionship during the experience of suffering or a theoretical question about whether or not God exists? Would our neighbors be able to recognize the difference between good and evil if God did not provide a standard via his general revelation?

5. What do people have to know in order to be able to recognize real love, as Jesus described the topic in John 13:35? How do people know what real love is? What is happening when people recognize the moral authority of biblical commandments?

6. What is a false absolute? What are some examples? What is the role of false absolutes in ideologies? In education? What is a good Christian response?

7. Why are there different types of secular ethical theories? To what extent and how should Christians use secular ethical theories? Are these theories really developed without God?

About the Author

Biography

Thomas K. Johnson received his Ph.D. in ethics and philosophical theology from the University of Iowa (USA, 1987) after a research fellowship at Eberhard-Karls Universität (Tübingen, Germany). He received a Master of Divinity (*Magna Cum Laude*) from Covenant Theological Seminary (St. Louis, USA, 1981), and a BA from Hope College (Michigan, USA, 1977).

After serving as a church planter in the Presbyterian Church in America, he became a visiting professor of philosophy at the European Humanities University (EHU) in Minsk, Belarus, 1994–1996. (EHU is a dissident, anti-Communist university, forced into exile by the Belarusian dictator in 2004.)

Since 1996 Johnson and his wife have lived in Prague, where he taught philosophy at Anglo-American University (four years) and at Charles University (eight years). From 2004 to 2013 he was director of the Comenius Institute in Prague, which works to develop Czech Christian academic spokespeople. He began teaching apologetics, ethics, and theology for Martin Bucer Seminary in 2003 and has taught theology and philosophy in eleven universities or theological schools in nine countries.

Johnson is presently Vice President for Research, Martin Bucer European School of Theology and Research Institutes; Special Advisor to the International Institute for Religious Freedom (WEA); Professor of Philosophy, Global Scholars; ordained minister, Presbyterian Church in America; and Senior Advisor to the Theological Commission of the World Evangelical Alliance. In March, 2016, he was appointed Religious Freedom Ambassador to the Vatican, representing the World Evangelical Alliance and its 600 million members.

His wife, Leslie P. Johnson, was Director of the Christian International School of Prague, 2004-2015. She is currently an educational consultant affiliated with the Association of Christian Schools International. They have three married children and several grandchildren.

Publications by Dr. Johnson; for most of these materials you can click on the titles to read or download the texts. If you are reading in a printed version, a simple internet search should lead you to most of these titles.

Publications by Thomas K. Johnson which are readily available online, in libraries, or from the publisher:[117]

1. Books

Natural Law Ethics: An Evangelical Proposal, volume 6 in the Christian Philosophy Today series (Bonn: VKW, 2005).

What Difference Does the Trinity Make? A Complete Faith, Life, and Worldview, volume 7 in the Global Issues Series of the World Evangelical Alliance (Bonn: VKW, 2009).

The First Step in Missions Training: How Our Neighbors Are Wrestling with God's General Revelation, volume 1 in the World of Theology series published by the Theological Commission of the World Evangelical Alliance (Bonn: VKW, 2014).

Christian Ethics in Secular Cultures, volume 2 in the World of Theology series published by the Theological Commission of the World Evangelical Alliance (Bonn: VKW, 2014).

Human Rights: A Christian Primer, second edition, volume 1 in the Global Issues Series of the World Evangelical Alliance (Bonn: VKW, 2016).

Creation Care and Loving our Neighbors, with Thomas Schirrmacher, volume 17 in the Global Issues Series of the World Evangelical Alliance (Bonn: VKW, 2016).

Global Declarations on Freedom of Religion or Belief and Human Rights, selected and edited by Thomas K. Johnson with Thomas Schirrmacher and Christof Sauer, volume 18 in the Global Issues Series of the World Evangelical Alliance (Bonn: VKW, 2017).

Two of the book series of the World Evangelical Alliance in which Dr. Johnson is an editor, the *World of Theology* series published by the Theological Commission and the *Global Issues* series published by the International Institute for Religious Freedom, are available as free downloads here.

2. WEA Statements

The Bad Urach Call: Toward understanding suffering, persecution, and martyrdom for the global church in mission, 2010. This is a call to action ad-

---

[117] Several people have very kindly given their time and energy to assist with this publishing program. These include Ruth Baldwin, Dr. Johnson's primary editing assistant, along with John Colley, Russ Johnson, Patricia Foster, Anke Damson, and Bob Hussey.

dressed to the global evangelical movement which summarizes the larger Bad Urach Statement.

"Xenophobia, Hospitality, and the Refugee Crisis in Europe," September, 2015.

Dr. Johnson was the primary author of Efraim Tendero's speech on "The Gospel and Religious Extremism," March, 2016.

3. Booklets and essays on the WEA website

Adam and Eve, Who Are You? 2004.

Deceptive Philosophy, 2004.

Human Rights and Christian Ethics, 2005.

Progress, Knowledge, and God, 2005.

Interpreting the Ten Commandments: A Study in Special Hermeneutics, 2005.

Sex, Marriage, and Science, 2005.

Paul's Intellectual Courage in the Face of Sophisticated Unbelief, 2006.

Christ and Culture, 2007.

Biblical Principles in the Public Square: Theological Foundations for Christian Civic Participation, 2008.

Foundational Political Values to Guide Governmental and Family Care of Children, 2008.

What Makes Sex So Special? 2009.

The Moral Crisis of the West, 2009.

The Spirit of the Protestant Work Ethic and the World Economic Crisis, 2009.

Human Rights and the Human Quest, 2009.

Rights, Religions, and Ideologies, 2009.

Law and Gospel: The Hermeneutical/Homiletical Key to Reformation Theology and Ethics, 2009.

Triple Knowledge and the Reformation Faith, 2009.

"Thinking Twice about the Minaret Ban in Switzerland," 2009.

"Why Evangelicals Need a Code of Ethics for Missions," with Thomas Schirrmacher, 2010.

Translated, edited, and expanded "Defection from Islam: A Disturbing Human Rights Dilemma" by Christine Schirrmacher, 2010.

Translated and edited "Islamic Human Rights Declarations and Their Critics" by Christine Schirrmacher, 2011.

"In Context: Christian Witness in a Multi-Religious World: Recommendations for Conduct," 2011.

Sabbath, Work, and the Quest for Meaning, 2011.

Education and the Human Quest: The Correlation of Existence and History, 2011.

"May Christians Go to Court?" With Thomas Schirrmacher, 2011.

Dutch Reformed Philosophy in North America: Three Varieties in the Late Twentieth Century, 2012.

The Protester, the Dissident, and the Christian, 2012.

4. Other booklets and essays available online

"That Which Is Noteworthy and That Which Is Astonishing in the Global Charter of Conscience," IJRF 5:1, 2012, 7-9.

"Religious Freedom and the Twofold Work of God in the World," IJRF 6:1/2 2013, 17-24.

"Dualisms, Dualities, and Creation Care," with Thomas Schirrmacher, World Reformed Fellowship, November, 2013.

Dialogue with Kierkegaard in Protestant Theology: Donald Bloesch, Francis Schaeffer, and Helmut Thielicke, MBS Text 175, 2013.

The Trinity in the Bible and Selected Creeds of the Church, MBS Text 179, 2013.

Foreword entitled "The Holistic Mission of William Carey," in *William Carey: Theologian – Linguist – Social Reformer,* edited by Thomas Schirrmacher, volume 4 in the World of Theology Series of the WEA Theological Commission, 2013.

"The Crisis of Modernity and the Task of Moral Philosophy," World Reformed Fellowship, April, 2014.

"Faith and Reason Active in Love: The Theology of Creation Care," with Thomas Schirrmacher, World Reformed Fellowship, May, 2014.

"The Church's Complex Relationship with the Idea of Wealth and Need," a speech given at the Pontifical Academy of Social Sciences, the Vatican, June, 2014, published by the World Reformed Fellowship.

"Why Is Religious Extremism So Attractive? Life Together and the Search for Meaning," IJRF, vol. 7 1/2, 2014, 9-12.

Family/Sexual Chaos and the Evangelical Faith, November, 2014, a booklet prepared on behalf of the Theological Commission of the World Evangelical Alliance and submitted to the Vatican Synod on the Family, published by the World Reformed Fellowship.

"Lessons from Paris 2015: Clash of Civilizations or Battling Nihilisms?" published by the World Reformed Fellowship, January, 2015.

Foreword entitled, "The Moral Structure of the Condemnation of Slavery in Amos," in *The Humanisation of Slavery in the Old Testament*, edited by Thomas Schirrmacher, volume 8 in the World of Theology Series of the WEA Theological Commission, 2015.

"Religious Terrorism, Brussels, and the Search for Meaning," *Evangelical Focus*, 29 March, 2016.

"Addressing the Scars on the Face of Christendom," World Reformed Fellowship, September 23, 2016.

Learning to Love the Persecuted Church, MBS Text 186, 2016.

Why is the Virgin Birth so Important? MBS Text 187, 2017.

Poverty and Chastity in Reformed Ethics MBS Text 188, 2017.

With Thomas Schirrmacher, "Let the Reformation Continue!" World Reformed Fellowship, March 26, 2017.

5. Books edited by Dr. Johnson

Edited and wrote a foreword entitled "The Bible and Global Social Problems," Thomas Schirrmacher, *Racism, With an Essay by Richard Howell on Caste in India,* the WEA Global Issues Series, volume 8, 2011.

Edited and wrote a foreword entitled "The Father of Modern Education," Jan Habl, *Lessons in Humanity: From the Life and Work of Jan Amos Komensky,* 2011, on the WEA CD zip file found at http://www.bucer.de/ressourcen/wea-cd.html.

Christine Schirrmacher, *The Sharia: Law and Order in Islam,* the WEA Global Issues Series, volume 10, 2013.

Thomas Schirrmacher, *Human Trafficking: The Return to Slavery,* the WEA Global Issues Series, volume 12, 2013.

Edited and wrote a foreword entitled "Ethics for Christians in the World," Thomas Schirrmacher, *Leadership and Ethical Responsibility: The Three Aspect of Every Decision,* the WEA Global Issues Series, volume 13, 2013.

Thomas Schirrmacher, *Fundamentalism: When Religion Becomes Dangerous,* the WEA Global Issues Series, volume 14, 2013.

Thomas Schirrmacher, *Advocate of Love: Martin Bucer as Theologian and Pastor,* volume 5 in the World of Theology Series, 2013.

Thomas Schirrmacher, *Culture of Shame/Culture of Guilt,* volume 6 in the World of Theology Series, 2013.

Edited and revised Thomas Schirrmacher, *The Koran and the Bible,* volume 7 in the World of Theology Series, 2013.

Ken Gnanakan, *Responsible Stewardship of God's Creation,* the WEA Global Issues Series, volume 11, 2014.

Edited and wrote a foreword entitled "The Holocaust and German Thought on Human Rights," Thomas Schirrmacher, *Human Rights: Promise and Reality,* the WEA Global Issues Series, volume 15, 2014.

Edited and wrote a foreword for Jan Habl, *Teaching and Learning Through Story: Comenius' Labyrinth and the Educational Potential of Narrative Allegory,* 2014, on the WEA CD zip file found at http://www.bucer.de/ressourcen/wea-cd.html.

Christine Schirrmacher, *Political Islam: When Faith Turns Out to Be Politics*, the WEA Global Issues Series, volume 16, 2016. http://www.bucer.org/uploads/tx_org/WEA_GIS_16_Christine_Schirrmacher_-_Political_Islam.pdf.

World Evangelical Alliance

World Evangelical Alliance is a global ministry working with local churches around the world to join in common concern to live and proclaim the Good News of Jesus in their communities. WEA is a network of churches in 129 nations that have each formed an evangelical alliance and over 100 international organizations joining together to give a worldwide identity, voice and platform to more than 600 million evangelical Christians. Seeking holiness, justice and renewal at every level of society – individual, family, community and culture, God is glorified and the nations of the earth are forever transformed.

Christians from ten countries met in London in 1846 for the purpose of launching, in their own words, "a new thing in church history, a definite organization for the expression of unity amongst Christian individuals belonging to different churches." This was the beginning of a vision that was fulfilled in 1951 when believers from 21 countries officially formed the World Evangelical Fellowship. Today, 150 years after the London gathering, WEA is a dynamic global structure for unity and action that embraces 600 million evangelicals in 129 countries. It is a unity based on the historic Christian faith expressed in the evangelical tradition. And it looks to the future with vision to accomplish God's purposes in discipling the nations for Jesus Christ.

Commissions:

- Theology
- Missions
- Religious Liberty
- Women's Concerns
- Youth
- Information Technology

Initiatives and Activities

- Ambassador for Human Rights
- Ambassador for Refugees
- Creation Care Task Force
- Global Generosity Network
- International Institute for Religious Freedom
- International Institute for Islamic Studies
- Leadership Institute
- Micah Challenge
- Global Human Trafficking Task Force
- Peace and Reconciliation Initiative
- UN-Team

Church Street Station
P.O. Box 3402
New York, NY 10008-3402
Phone +[1] 212 233 3046
Fax +[1] 646-957-9218
www.worldea.org

Giving Hands

GIVING HANDS GERMANY (GH) was established in 1995 and is officially recognized as a nonprofit foreign aid organization. It is an international operating charity that – up to now – has been supporting projects in about 40 countries on four continents. In particular we care for orphans and street children. Our major focus is on Africa and Central America. GIVING HANDS always mainly provides assistance for self-help and furthers human rights thinking.

The charity itself is not bound to any church, but on the spot we are co-operating with churches of all denominations. Naturally we also cooperate with other charities as well as governmental organizations to provide assistance as effective as possible under the given circumstances.

The work of GIVING HANDS GERMANY is controlled by a supervisory board. Members of this board are Manfred Feldmann, Colonel V. Doner and Kathleen McCall. Dr. Christine Schirrmacher is registered as legal manager of GIVING HANDS at the local district court. The local office and work of the charity are coordinated by Rev. Horst J. Kreie as executive manager. Dr. theol. Thomas Schirrmacher serves as a special consultant for all projects.

Thanks to our international contacts companies and organizations from many countries time and again provide containers with gifts in kind which we send to the different destinations where these goods help to satisfy elementary needs. This statutory purpose is put into practice by granting nutrition, clothing, education, construction and maintenance of training centers at home and abroad, construction of wells and operation of water treatment systems, guidance for self-help and transportation of goods and gifts to areas and countries where needy people live.

GIVING HANDS has a publishing arm under the leadership of Titus Vogt, that publishes human rights and other books in English, Spanish, Swahili and other languages.

These aims are aspired to the glory of the Lord according to the basic Christian principles put down in the Holy Bible.

Baumschulallee 3a • D-53115 Bonn • Germany
Phone: +49 / 228 / 695531 • Fax +49 / 228 / 695532
www.gebende-haende.de • info@gebende-haende.de

 # Martin Bucer Seminary

Faithful to biblical truth
Cooperating with the Evangelical Alliance
Reformed

Solid training for the Kingdom of God
- Alternative theological education
- Study while serving a church or working another job
- Enables students to remain in their own churches
- Encourages independent thinking
- Learning from the growth of the universal church.

Academic
- For the Bachelor's degree: 180 Bologna-Credits
- For the Master's degree: 120 additional Credits
- Both old and new teaching methods: All day seminars, independent study, term papers, etc.

Our Orientation:
- Complete trust in the reliability of the Bible
- Building on reformation theology
- Based on the confession of the German Evangelical Alliance
- Open for innovations in the Kingdom of God

Our Emphasis:
- The Bible
- Ethics and Basic Theology
- Missions
- The Church

Our Style:
- Innovative
- Relevant to society
- International
- Research oriented
- Interdisciplinary

Structure
- 15 study centers in 7 countries with local partners
- 5 research institutes
- President: Prof. Dr. Thomas Schirrmacher
  Vice President: Prof. Dr. Thomas K. Johnson
- Deans: Thomas Kinker, Th.D.;
  Titus Vogt, lic. theol., Carsten Friedrich, M.Th.

Missions through research
- Institute for Religious Freedom
- Institute for Islamic Studies
- Institute for Life and Family Studies
- Institute for Crisis, Dying, and Grief Counseling
- Institute for Pastoral Care

www.bucer.eu • info@bucer.eu

Berlin I Bielefeld I Bonn I Chemnitz I Hamburg I Munich I Pforzheim
Innsbruck I Istanbul I Izmir I Linz I Prague I São Paulo I Tirana I Zurich

www.ingramcontent.com/pod-product-compliance
Lightning Source LLC
Chambersburg PA
CBHW071438160426
43195CB00013B/1955